FAMOUS SEA BATTLES

Donald Macintyre

Hamlyn

London · New York · Sydney · Toronto

The dates given in this book are those which conform to the
present day calendar

First published 1974

The Hamlyn Publishing Group Limited
London · New York · Sydney · Toronto
Astronaut House, Feltham, Middlesex, England

© Copyright 1974 The Hamlyn Publishing Group Limited

ISBN 0 600 38066 1

Printed by Litografía A. Romero, S. A.
Tenerife (Spain). D. L. 321 - 74

Contents

The Battle of Lepanto

17 October 1571

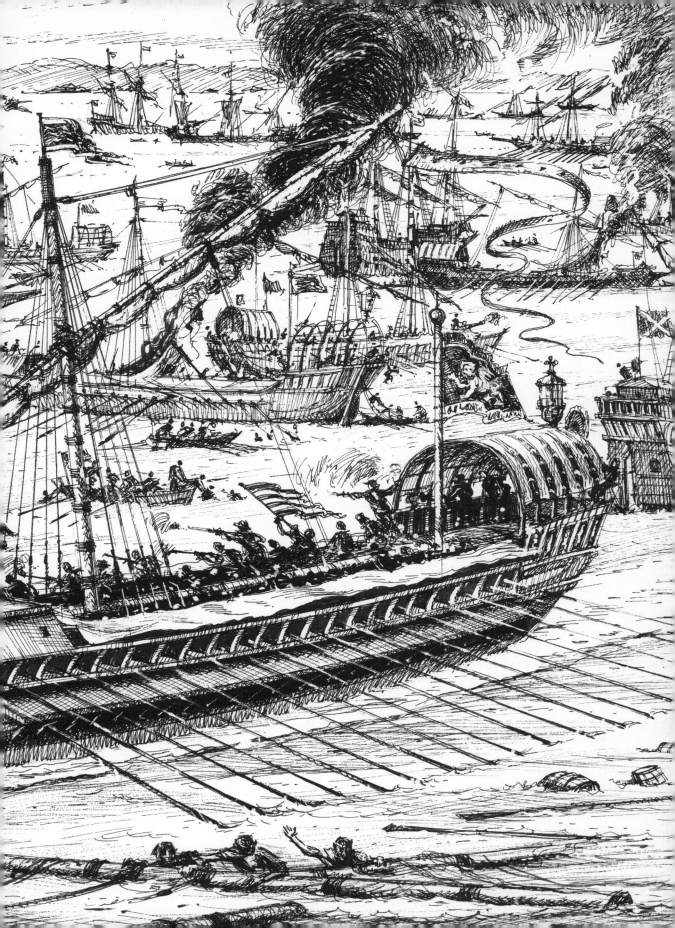

The blue waters of the Gulf of Patras, which lies between the mainland of Greece and its southern peninsula, the Morea, sparkled under the clear autumn sky. The sun shone on two long lines of ships, their sails lowered and stowed. Banks of long oars, or sweeps, projected from the sides of the ships as they moved into position abreast of one another like starters in a rowing race.

But this was no regatta. It was mid-day on 17 October 1571 and a decisive battle between the fleet of the Turkish Sultan and that of the Holy League—Spain, the Papal Dominions and the Republic of Venice—was about to begin. It was to decide whether the control of the Mediterranean by the Arabs, led by Turkey, which had been growing rapidly over the last sixty years, should continue. It was also to be the last full-scale battle between galleys—warships propelled by oars. Sailing warships, or galleons, were already proving themselves superior in other seas.

The Ottoman Turks, a warlike Mohammedan race, had invaded Europe from Asia Minor. In 1453 they captured Constantinople, capital of the Eastern Roman empire, after a long siege, and made it their own.

After the fall of Constantinople, this Ottoman empire stretched from what is now Romania to the Euphrates. In 1512, Syria and Egypt fell to the Turks. Under Suleiman I—the Magnificent—(1520–1566), the Ottoman empire expanded still further into Europe. Suleiman's armies were besieging Vienna itself and when the Mohammedan corsairs of the Barbary coast of North Africa gave him their allegiance, the Ottoman Turks became stronger at sea than any one of the Christian countries of the Mediterranean.

Year after year, Turkish galley fleets ravaged the coasts of Italy, France and Spain, sacking towns and carrying off the inhabitants as slaves.

The Christian Mediterranean states were often too engaged in fighting other European countries to pay attention to the menace from the East. But they finally took alarm when first Malta (1568) and then Cyprus (1570) were besieged. Then at the appeal of Pope Pius V, a league was formed by Spain, Venice, Genoa, Savoy and the various princes of Italy. These included the Pope himself, who in those days had great secular power as ruler of the Papal States.

It was agreed to assemble a large combined naval force to combat the Turkish fleet. Half the cost was to be borne by Philip II of Spain, one-third by Venice, the remainder subscribing according to their means. To command it, the Pope selected Don John of Austria, the handsome, brave and courtly half-brother of Philip II. He had already shown himself to be a skilled commander at sea in skirmishes against the Barbary pirates; and on land in repressing the insurrection of Philip's Moorish subjects in Granada. Second-in-command would be the Prince Marco Antonio Colonna who, as 'Admiral of the Church', was to lead the Papal force. Sebastiano Veniero would be in command of the largest naval contingent, the Venetian fleet of more than one hundred and ten ships. A veteran of seventy years of age and of numerous campaigns, he had a reputation for valour and vigour. His fierce patriotism inspired a burning desire to destroy the heathen power that was driving his great city-state to her commercial ruin.

Naval forces at that time were composed

mainly of galleys. These ships were propelled in battle or in calm weather by oars, usually pulled by slaves and convicted criminals, although there were volunteer members of the crews. If the wind served while on passage from one place to another, triangular lateen sails could be hoisted on two masts.

Each galley was armed with five large cannon in the bow, which would be fired as the ship approached its opponent bow-on. Soldiers in platforms raised up at bow and stern would add the fire of their 'arquebuses', an early type of firearm or, in the case of the Turks, of their bows and arrows. Then the galley would attempt to thrust its iron-shod underwater ram into its opponent. If this failed, the two ships would be run alongside each other and hand-to-hand fighting would break out between the opposing soldiers wielding swords and pikes. European galleys were about 150 feet long; they had twenty oars on either side manned by two hundred rowers. The Turkish vessels were a little different in their design.

Another type of European fighting ship, of which Don John had six, was the galleass—a very large galley of some 1,500 tons, with tall fore and aft 'castles', and mounting some thirty cannon. They were propelled by four hundred and fifty rowers and the crew totalled about a thousand men.

Agreement by the League on the force was one thing; to assemble it in good time at Messina, the selected port, was quite another. Not until 26 September 1571, nearly four months after the founding of the League, did its fleet finally assemble; and on the 27th Don John reviewed it—one hundred and six galleys of Venice, twelve of the Papal States and ninety more from

Right:
This map is taken from a contemporary engraving showing the disposition of the Turkish and Christian fleets, the number of ships involved and the names of the commanders.

Spain and her dependent or allied states – two hundred and eight galleys in all and six galleasses. It was not one moment too soon; a mere 240 miles away, across the Ionian Sea at Corfu was the whole Turkish fleet of some two hundred and seventy galleys under the Sultan's admiral, Ali Pasha.

Until the middle of August, Ali Pasha had paid scant attention to the rumours of the League's preparations for war; he had continued to occupy himself with war against Venice by attacking and capturing a number of Venetian settlements on the Adriatic coast. While besieging Cattaro (today Kotor) and Ragusa (today Dubrovnik), news came of the Christian concentration at Messina. Ali Pasha at once raised the sieges and sailed south to concentrate his fleet at Corfu.

On 20 September, a courier from the Sultan brought him orders to concentrate all his efforts on fighting and destroying the Christian fleet. He retired, therefore, to the anchorage of Lepanto (today called Navpaktos) on the northern shore of the Gulf of Patras. Here, he made preparations that included the embarkation of soldiers which brought their total to 25,000.

By this time Don John of Austria's great fleet had begun its advance to meet the Turks. His desire to press on with all speed and bring the enemy to action was held in check by the councils of war he was bound to call before making any decision. However, by 6 October the fleet had advanced by easy stages to anchor in Corfu harbour and it was there that Don John at last got firm news on 10 October that the enemy was assembled at Lepanto.

He decided not to waste any time and to advance as soon as possible to the attack.

Bad weather caused some delay, but by the dawn of 17 October the fleet was approaching Cape Scropha at the entrance to the Gulf of Patras. As the Cape fell back on their port side and the waters of the Gulf opened to their view, a dense cloud of white and coloured sails was revealed. It was the enemy fleet. Asked if he wanted to call a council of war, Don John replied – no doubt with a feeling of relief – 'The time for councils has passed: now it's time to fight.' The beat of drums summoned the crews to action stations, and the great banner of the League, blessed by the Pope, was hoisted to the masthead of Don John's flagship.

Both fleets were organised in three divisions. The left wing of the Christian fleet and so the nearest to the northern shore of the Gulf, was composed of fifty-three galleys under the Venetian, Agostino Barbarigo. In the centre, the main body of sixty-two galleys under Don John himself, included the flagship of his second-in-command, Colonna, that of Veniero and of many of the most notable figures of Spain and the Holy Roman empire. The right wing of fifty-seven galleys was under the command of the Genoese, Giovanni Andrea Doria, son of Genoa's famous admiral, Andrea Doria.

Seven of this number under the Spaniard, Juan de Cardona were still behind, trying to reach their station on the extreme right, when the Christian ships all turned together to form line abreast to advance head-on against the enemy fleet which was similarly arrayed. Further back still was the reserve of thirty galleys under the Spanish Marquis of Santa Cruz. Finally there were the six galleasses whose station was in advance, two ahead of each of the three wings.

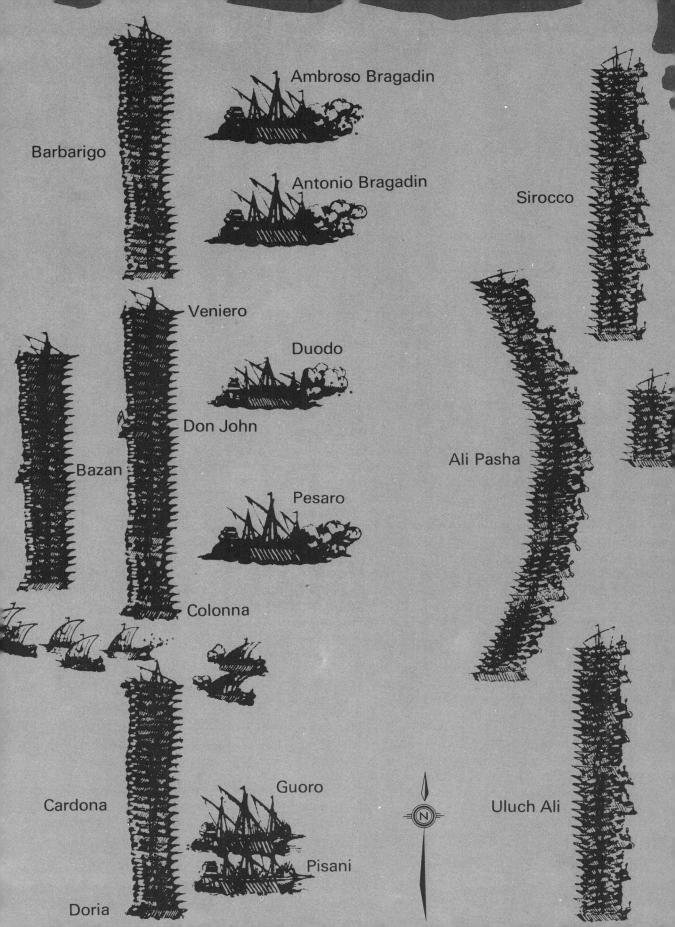

Ali Pasha's fleet had numerical superiority over his opponent's. His fleet consisted of two hundred and ten large galleys and sixty-three smaller galleys introduced by the Barbary corsairs and called galiotes or fustes. His soldiers were armed mainly with the bow and arrow rather than the arquebus, and most of his galleys were smaller than those of the Holy League. Thus Turkish superiority over the Christian fleet was more apparent than real.

Like their opponents, the Turks were arrayed in three divisions. The right, opposing Barbarigo, was composed of fifty-four galleys and two galiotes and commanded by Chulout, the Bey of Alexandria, familiarly known as 'Scirocco'.

With Ali Pasha in the centre, as in his opponent's fleet, was a glittering gathering of his notables, generals and corsair commanders. This division totalled eighty-seven galleys and eight galiotes. On the left, facing Doria, was Ali Pasha's lieutenant, Uluch Ali, the Bey of Algiers, with sixty-one galleys and thirty-two galiotes. The remainder of the galiotes (twenty-one) and eight galleys made up the reserve. The whole naval power of Turkey was present on this decisive day, with squadrons from Tripoli, Algiers, Rhodes, Anatolia, Alexandria and Syria as well as from Constantinople, the capital.

Both sides, on sighting the enemy, had lowered their sails and manoeuvred into station under oars. At noon the clarion call of Don John's trumpets sounded the charge, the banks of oars flashed in the sunlight and their blades cleaved the blue waters. As one, the rowers of either side under the lash of the slave masters, threw themselves into their agonising labour to the rhythm beaten on the drum. With the white froth of waves curling high from the bows, the galleys raced for their opponents, intent on thrusting their rams destructively into their hulls.

So, at least in the northern and central sections, the battle began. In the southern section the situation was different as will be seen in a moment. The first wings to clash were the northerly: Barbarigo's Venetians and Scirocco's Alexandrians. The two sides were roughly equal in number but the Christians had the advantage of larger ships, of greater cannon power and of fire-arms. Though Barbarigo fell mortally wounded with an arrow in his eye during the first exchange of fire, in the wild confusion that followed as the opposing ships crashed together, it was the Turks who were first repulsed as they tried, scimitar in hand, to board.

Then the Turks, in their turn, were overwhelmed and taken by assault. When Scirocco was killed and his body thrown into the sea, many of the Turkish galleys fled and ran themselves ashore. A massacre followed; by 2 o'clock in the afternoon the right wing of the Turkish fleet had ceased to exist.

In the centre, as the two sides steered for one another at full speed, the two Venetian galleasses out in front brought their cannon-fire into good use, badly damaging some of the leading Turkish galleys. This caused panic in the Ottoman line; some galleys ceased rowing or even backed water with their oars; the Turkish superiority in numbers was offset by this confusion and loss of confidence. Ali Pasha's flagship shot out in front and for a while was unsupported.

In the wild fights that followed between individual ships, the Turkish galleys were

one after another destroyed or captured. Even so, Don John's flagship came near to being captured by that of Ali Pasha after Ali's ram had pierced his opponent as deeply as the fourth bench of rowers. Only when the Prince Colonna's galley, having captured that of the Turkish Bey of Negropont and having sent another to the bottom with its ram, arrived in support of the Christian flagship, was the issue decided; Ali Pasha and five hundred of his men were killed and his ship captured.

Thus two-thirds of the Turkish fleet had been totally overwhelmed; but in the south a different situation had arisen. There the fifty galleys of Doria (Cardona's seven had still not taken up station in the line) were opposed by Uluch Ali's sixty-one galleys and thirty-two galiotes. The longer Turkish line overlapped Doria's and when it began to threaten to outflank and encircle his right wing, Doria turned south in line ahead to prevent this.

For a while both sides steered south, away from the main battle; but then Uluch, having deliberately or by chance drawn Doria off, reversed course and before Doria could do the same, fell on the right flank of the Christian centre. For a time he had great success: amongst the galleys taken or destroyed was that of the Grand Prior of Malta, Giustiniani.

From all sides, however, help for the hard-pressed Christian galleys was on its way. Cardona, at last arriving to take station, was followed by Santa Cruz's thirty ships of the reserve. Don John himself, seeing the crisis occurring, left his prizes and with a dozen galleys of the centre threw himself into the fight. Lastly Doria's still fresh ships arrived; Uluch saw that his gallant effort had failed; with thirteen

of his galleys he escaped northwards up the Greek coast; thirty other Turkish units limped away to take shelter in Lepanto.

By sundown the Turkish naval power had ceased to exist. One hundred and ninety galleys had been captured; fifteen had been sunk or burnt; 20,000 Turks or Arabs had died. On the side of the League, 7,500 men had been killed and fifteen of their galleys had been destroyed.

Nearly three hundred years were to pass before a Turkish fleet again tried to dominate the Mediterranean. Then it was a combined British, French and Russian fleet which in 1827 defeated it at Navarino— the last battle fought wholly under sail, less than a hundred miles from the scene of the Battle of Lepanto.

The Defeat of the Spanish Armada

July-August 1588

Previous Page:
The *Ark Royal,* an example of the new English
Galleon. Originally laid down for Sir Walter
Raleigh, The *Ark Royal* was Howard's flagship
during the Armada campaign.

It was the afternoon of 29 July 1588. On
Plymouth Hoe, the flat cliff-top which
looks out over the Sound, there was a scene
both splendid and homely. Playing the old
country game of bowls were Lord Howard
of Effingham (the Lord Admiral of
England), Sir Francis Drake, England's
greatest sailor and scourge of the
Spaniards, and John Hawkins, Comp-
troller of the Queen's Navy. Hawkins was
responsible for the new, improved type of
galleon, the man-of-war, which was the
navy's backbone. A gentle south-west
breeze blew while summer sunshine flooded
the green.

Drake, according to tradition, was
hefting a bowl and about to play, when a
breathless figure burst on the scene
demanding his attention. It was Captain
Fleming of the bark *Golden Hind,* one of
a screen of scouting ships which had been
deployed in the Channel approaches. He
had sighted a large group of Spanish ships
lying-to off the Scilly Islands, waiting
evidently for others to join them. Under a
press of sail, Fleming had sped back to
Plymouth to report that the long-expected
'Invincible Armada' of Spain had at last
appeared. This was electrifying news: but
according to the legend, Drake's response
was the calm statement: 'We have time
enough to finish the game and beat the
Spaniards, too.'

And, indeed, as Drake well knew, sailing
ships could not beat out of Plymouth
against both a south-west wind and the
flood-tide that was running. Not until
10 o'clock that night did the English fleet
begin to work their way out to an anchorage
under the lee of Rame Head. On the following morning, Howard's flagship, *Ark Royal,*
with the royal standard at the masthead,

the *Revenge,* wearing Drake's Vice-
Admiral's flag, Hawkins' galleon, *Victory*
and Martin Frobisher's *Triumph*–biggest
of the fleet at 1,100 tons–led fifty-seven
ships out into the Channel. That afternoon
they caught their first sight of the enemy,
a daunting forest of masts on the western
horizon. A new era in naval warfare
between sailing fleets such as the world
had never before seen, was about to begin.

The Armada had been in preparation
for some years under the guidance of King
Philip II of Spain's Captain-General of the
Ocean Sea, the Marquis of Santa Cruz who
had commanded a Spanish squadron of
galleys at Lepanto. Its backbone was
Philip's fighting navy–ten galleons of
Portugal, ten of Castile with four large
well-armed West Indiamen and four
galleasses (the hybrid rowing and sailing
ships seen at Lepanto). In addition there
were four squadrons, each of ten large
armed merchant ships, more than thirty
light craft to act as dispatch boats and
screen. Finally there was an unwieldy
block of twenty-three *urcas* (freighters,
store-ships, etc.). The Armada's task was to
sweep up Channel, make rendezvous with
Parma's dreaded army of the Netherlands,
embarked in barges, and escort the whole
force across to a landing near Margate.

For Philip II, champion of the Roman
Catholic cause in a Europe divided between
bitterly hostile Catholics and Protestants,
had decided that only through conquest
could England be led back into religious
subservience to the Pope. He had been
married in his youth to Catholic Queen
Mary Tudor of England. After her death,
he had for many years pinned his hopes on
a rebellion by English Catholics to put
Mary, Queen of Scots on the throne in

THE SPANISH ARMADA

Left, from Top to Bottom:
The Duke of Medina Sidonia
Sir John Hawkins
Sir Francis Drake
Lord Howard of Effingham

place of Protestant Elizabeth. But these hopes had been finally destroyed when Elizabeth, after holding Mary prisoner for nineteen years, had her executed on 8 February 1587.

The 'Enterprise of England', as the Armada campaign was called, had been intended for the summer of 1587. But preparations for it had been completely disrupted when Drake led a squadron to 'singe the King of Spain's beard', as he called it, by destroying the large assembly of shipping in the harbour of Cadiz at the end of April. During the following month, Drake hovered off Cape St. Vincent snapping up shipping carrying essential stores for the Armada to Lisbon. As a result of all this, the Enterprise had to be postponed for a year. In the interval the Marquis of Santa Cruz died, and was succeeded in command by the Duke of Medina Sidonia.

The Duke accepted the appointment with gloomy reluctance, protesting his inexperience of naval affairs. He met with every imaginable difficulty, delay and shortage, and it was not until 28 May 1588 that the Armada finally put to sea. Owing to contrary winds and storms, however, it was not until the end of the month that the whole fleet was clear of Lisbon harbour. Its progress was then painfully slow, beating against a northerly wind or wallowing becalmed. When store-ships failed to meet the fleet off Cape Finisterre, which was reached at the beginning of June, it was decided to put into Corunna for water, already running short. Half the fleet was caught outside the harbour by a violent storm, and it was not until 22 July that it set out again. On the 28th, soon after Captain Fleming saw its advance guard,

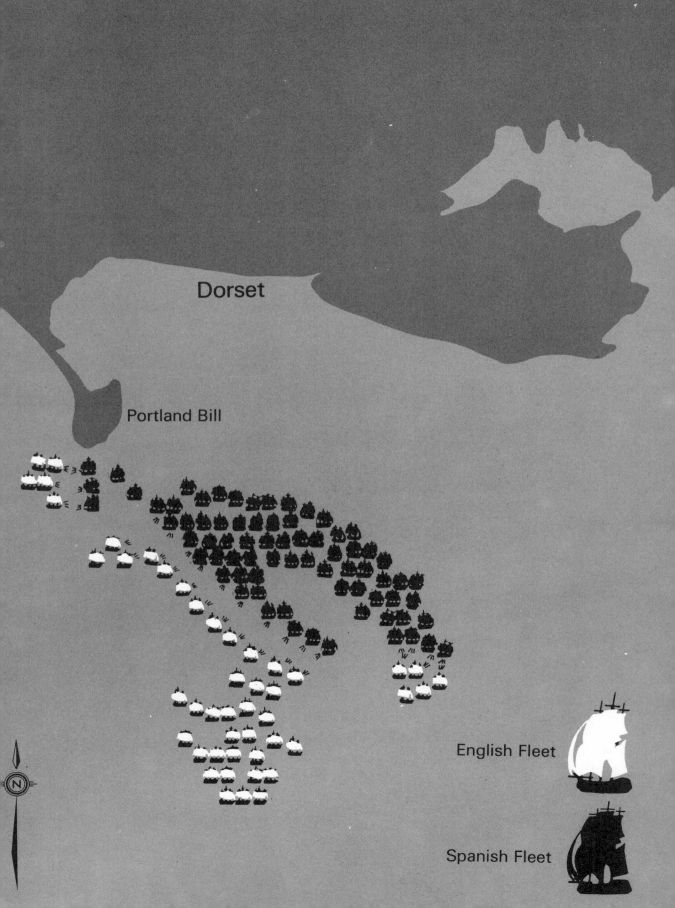

Dorset

Portland Bill

English Fleet

Spanish Fleet

Left:
This map is based on drawings by Robert Adams who died in 1595. The Armada, harried by the English fleet, has just passed Weymouth on Tuesday, 31 July 1588.

Overleaf:
An incident from the Battle of Gravelines. Drake is leading his squadron past the *San Martin* at point-blank range to pour in their broadsides.

it re-united off the Scillies. By the 29th, it was off the Lizard and advancing up Channel.

The English fleet to oppose the Armada was centred on eighteen powerful galleons of the new design, and seven smaller of between 100 and 300 tons. They would be supported by a swarm of merchantmen and light craft; but it would be on the galleons that the main fighting task would fall. These had been specially designed for the purpose in three ways. By increasing their length in comparison to breadth and by cutting down the tall fore and aft castles previously favoured, their sailing qualities had been greatly improved, particularly their ability to beat up wind. Then by decking-over their previously open waists, additional deck space was made available to mount a larger number of guns. And finally, in place of a few short-range, heavy-shotted 'cannons and demi-cannons' and a great many light guns for shooting at close range, broadsides of long 'culverins' or 'demi-culverins' were mounted.

With these guns an enemy, armed in the old fashion, could be engaged from outside the range of his cannon. And with their improved sailing qualities the new galleons could choose their own range, steadily break up the helpless enemy and break off action when they chose. This, at least, was the theory. All was yet to be tested in this new form of warfare.

To employ such tactics it was necessary to get to windward of the enemy. To gain the 'weather gauge' as this was called, the English ships beat, close-hauled, up wind. The Duke of Medina Sidonia followed suit to try to prevent it, only to discover for the first time the fine weatherly qualities Hawkins had managed to give to the new

galleons. By the morning of the 31st, the English were to windward. From the Duke of Medina Sidonia's flagship, the galleon *San Martin,* the puff of smoke of a signal cannon-shot drifted away; to her masthead was hoisted the sacred banner which had been dedicated with all the solemn ritual of the Catholic church before sailing from Lisbon. It was the signal for battle.

To understand the Spanish tactics from now on, it must be remembered that the Armada was not just a fighting fleet. It was a huge military convoy with twenty-three clumsy, fat-bellied *urcas* to be protected. Although armed, these ships were no match for galleons. As they advanced up Channel to the rendezvous with Parma, the Spanish fleet was formed in a great crescent. The *urcas* were in the centre, the fighting ships forming the two backward curving horns. In this formation, any ships attacking from the windward side must engage the well-armed ships in the horns. If they attempted to get at the centre they would find themselves surrounded and forced into a close-range mêlée in which the advantage of the new English galleons would be lost.

It was an immensely difficult formation for sailing ships, something which had never been attempted before. It is a measure of the fine seamanship of the Spanish and Portuguese that for the next six days, under repeated attack and in variable weather, they maintained it unbroken.

The first of these attacks now began as, on the left wing, Howard's *Ark Royal* led a line of galleons across the stern of the rearmost ship, the *Rata Coronada* of Don Alonso de Leiva. The Spaniard, followed by the huge carrack *Regazona,* largest ship of the Armada, turned in an effort to get to

close quarters; but Howard was able to keep his distance. No more than a long range exchange of broadsides took place, doing little damage to either side.

On the other wing, Drake's *Revenge* led the *Victory* and *Triumph* in a similar manoeuvre against the galleon, *San Juan de Portugal,* flagship of Vice-Admiral Juan Martinez de Recalde. He, too, swung round to present his broadside, but was not supported. Even so the English, following their chosen tactics, held off, cannonading and doing some minor damage for more than an hour; then when support finally came to the *San Juan,* they broke off the action.

So the first day ended with little damage done to either side as a result of the fighting. The English had found the enemy larger, tougher and more skilful than expected, and their own tactics less effective. The Spaniards were now to suffer their first casualties, however.

On the left centre of the crescent, the poop and stern castle of the large armed merchant ship, *San Salvador,* suddenly blew up as barrels of powder exploded. The ship burst into flames. Medina Sidonia halted the fleet while rescue operations took place and when the fires were under control, the *San Salvador* was towed in amongst the urcas. But she had been fatally damaged. On the following day the *San Salvador* was abandoned, apparently sinking, only to be picked up and towed as a prize into Weymouth Bay by Captain Fleming of the *Golden Hind.*

Another ship which was in trouble at this time, was the flagship of Pedro de Valdes, commanding the Andalusian squadron of armed merchantmen on the right wing. She had lost her bowsprit in a collision and had been taken in tow. Now, in a choppy sea and gusts of wind from varying directions, she was taken aback. Her unstayed foremast collapsed. Once again the fleet had to be stopped for rescue operations; but by late afternoon efforts to get her again in tow had been unsuccessful. At the urging of his Chief of Staff, Diego Flores de Valdes, cousin and bitter enemy of Pedro, the Duke waited no longer, leaving some minor units to give what help they could.

These, too, were forced to abandon Valdes, when in the last of the evening light, the English were seen approaching. Francis Drake's famous ability to be in the right place to pick up important prizes now served him well. The Spaniards believed *El Draque* had a magic mirror on which he could see the ships moving on all the seas of the world. Be that as it may, daybreak the next morning, 1 August, showed the crippled *Rosario* lying directly in the path of the *Revenge.* Pedro de Valdes lost little time in surrendering. He himself was taken aboard the *Revenge;* his ship was escorted, a prize, into Tor Bay.

For the next five days, the Invincible Armada made its way slowly up Channel before generally gentle, south-westerly breezes with intervals of summer calm. The English men-of-war snapped round its heels when any opportunity presented itself. Once or twice a shift of wind to an easterly quarter brought about a more general action. There was then a great thundering of guns amid drifting banks of smoke. The English tactics of keeping at long range achieved nothing decisive; but they caused a fair amount of damage and inflicted numerous casualties at little cost to themselves. The frustrated Spaniards

could do nothing to prevent this; and when, scornfully, they struck topsails and challenged their elusive enemies to close combat, the English refused to be drawn.

The Invincible Armada then resumed its defensive formation and its stately progress up Channel. Howard followed, ruefully reckoning his shortage of powder and shot, after expending so much for so little purpose. He did not realise that the Duke was equally worried on the same account.

No message had come from Parma with regard to a rendezvous. Medina Sidonia dare not let himself go through the Straits into the North Sea until such a meeting had been arranged. Late on 6 August, therefore, the whole Armada dropped anchor in Calais Roads while urgent messengers were sent ashore. The English, following close behind, promptly did the same.

The two great fleets thus lay barely a long culverin shot apart. Neither side could engage the other on the terms they wished to fight. From the English point of view, it was essential to keep the Armada moving.

And there was one way to do it. In those days of wooden ships and tarred ropes and rigging, the most feared occurrence at sea was fire. So, if a blazing, exploding ship were to be seen drifting down the wind towards one's anchor berth, unless it could be grappled by boats and towed clear, there was only one thing to do—cut one's cable and run for it.

The Spanish admiral had realised the danger; and when, after dark the next night, a line of flickering flame was seen to windward, leaping upwards as the rigging of the fireships was set ablaze, a screen of pinnaces was ready to receive and deal with them. Two of the monsters were grappled and towed clear. But when the loaded guns of the remainder began to explode as the flames reached them, the pinnace crews fled. Their panic spread to the Spanish fleet where ship after ship cut its cable and scattered seawards. Only the Duke's *San Martin* and four other galleons acted calmly; they slipped their anchor cables, marking them with buoys, and

27

shifted berth about one mile before re-anchoring.

Dawn on 8 August revealed to the English fleet none but these five ships and, close inshore, the flagship of the Spanish galleasses, the *San Lorenzo*, damaged as a result of collisions during the overnight confusion. Howard saw that, for the first time, the disciplined Spanish formation had been broken up. In response to the *Ark Royal's* signal gun, his whole fleet got under way. It had been joined by the squadron, including five royal galleons, under Lord Henry Seymour, which had been patrolling off the Flemish coast in case Parma tried to put to sea.

The English fleet had been organised into five squadrons. Four were led by Drake's *Revenge* to attack the *San Martin* and her consorts. The fifth squadron was Howard's and he took it shorewards where the *San Lorenzo*, now aground, was captured by the crews from a flotilla of his boats. She could never be refloated, however, and after having thoroughly looted her, Howard abandoned her and steered to join the brisk fight out at sea – the Battle of Gravelines as it is often called.

Drake had decided the time had come to fight at closer range and make every round of his scanty ammunition tell. He led his squadron past the *San Martin* at point-blank range to pour in their broadsides. He then left the other squadrons, led by Frobisher, Hawkins and Seymour, to continue battering the Spanish flagship. Drake's purpose was to disrupt the remainder of the Spaniards who were clawing their way off the Flemish shoals to leeward, trying to regain their formation.

Many of the Spanish ships suffered heavy damage and were near to sinking by mid-afternoon. On their decks, crowded with soldiers awaiting the opportunity to board, the slaughter was terrible.

The Armada, in great confusion, seemed for a time to be doomed to be cast away on the sandbanks of the Flanders coast. But it was saved by the onset of a furious squall of wind with sheets of blinding rain that brought fighting to a halt. Under its cover the Armada was able to disengage northwards. As the squall cleared, to the grudging admiration of its pursuers, the Armada was seen to regain its old impenetrable formation, shorten sail and offer to renew the battle.

But in fact the time for fighting was really past. Neither side had more than a few rounds of ammunition left for their large guns. It was the elements which were now to decide the fate of the Invincible Armada.

Howard, appealing urgently to the Queen's Minister, Walsingham, to send him supplies, did not yet realise this. 'Ever since morning,' he wrote that evening, 'we have chased them in fight until this evening late and distressed them much; but their fleet consisteth of mighty ships and great strength . . . and yet we pluck their feathers little and little.' Already during the squall, one of the large armed merchantmen had gone to the bottom. After dark, two galleons, the *San Mateo* and *San Felipe,* in a sinking condition, ran themselves aground and were snapped up by the Dutch flotilla penning the Duke of Parma in port. Early on the 9th another armed merchantman sank between the two fleets.

By this time, even sailing as close to the north-west gale as possible, the Armada was being slowly but surely driven to leeward on to the sand banks at the mouth of the River Scheldt. All the English had to do, it seemed, was to stand off and watch the enemy's destruction. To the Spanish only the celebration of Mass and Holy Communion in preparation for death remained. But then, when all hope had been abandoned, there came apparently in answer to their prayers, a miracle. The wind suddenly backed through some 67 degrees to west-south-west. The Armada was, for the moment, saved.

All it could now do, nevertheless, in the absence of an easterly wind to take it back through the Straits, was to try to get home to Spain taking the long route round the north of the British Isles. And as the south-westerly winds continued to blow, the two fleets sailed northwards for the next three days. When on 12 August they reached the latitude of the Firth of Forth, Howard was at last satisfied that no landing would be attempted. With food and water running short he turned away. Six days later his ships arrived in the various harbours of the Thames Estuary between Harwich and Margate.

That very day, Queen Elizabeth was at Tilbury inspecting the army that her Captain General, the Earl of Leicester, had managed to gather to oppose Parma, should he come. The following day she addressed her people in phrases that are amongst the best-remembered in English history: '. . . I am come amongst you as you see, at this time, not for my recreation and disport, but being resolved, in the midst and heat of the battle, to live or die amongst you all, and to lay down for my God and for my kingdom and for my people, my honour and my blood, even in the dust. I know I have the body of a weak and feeble woman, but I have the heart and stomach of a king, and of a king of England too, and think foul scorn that Parma or Spain, or any prince of Europe should dare to invade the borders of my realm; to which, rather than any dishonour shall grow by me, I myself will take up arms, I myself will be your general, judge, and rewarder of every one of your virtues in the field . . .'

It was a splendid, heroic speech, greeted with a roar of applause. But in fact, Elizabeth's sailors had already removed the possibility of battle when they chased the shattered Armada into the Norwegian Sea. To get home to Spain, in their battered and leaking ships, was the only ambition left to Medina Sidonia and his men. Almost every day saw ships break away or straggle from the main body, never to be heard of again. In typical, south-westerly storms of the North Atlantic, the Armada was largely scattered after passing north of the Shetlands. Ship after ship was wrecked on the Irish coast. The *San Martin* herself finally reached Santander on 23 September; sixty-six others reached various Spanish harbours in the next few days; and only one more before the end of the year. More than sixty ships had been lost. Of some 30,000 Spaniards who had sailed in the Invincible Armada, only 9,000 got home to Spain.

*   *   *

The defeat of the Spanish Armada did not decide the outcome of the war between Spain and England. That, in fact, smouldered on for another fifteen years. But, as victory by Britain's Navy was to bring about again and again in the 350 years to follow, it removed the threat of invasion and conquest by a greatly superior land power.

The Four Days' Battle

11-14 June 1666

Three times during the seventeenth century the English and Dutch waged naval wars against each other. They were fought to decide which nation should have the greatest share in the sea-trade of the world.

When ocean-going sailing ships were first developed in the fifteenth century, it was the Spanish and Portuguese who were the first to use them to much profit. They sent out explorers to discover the Americas to the west and a route around Africa to the fabled Indies to the east. To avoid disputes between the two nations, Pope Alexander VI established a line from pole to pole, to the west of which all newly-acquired lands were to be Spanish; to the east they were to be Portuguese.

This had blandly ignored the rights not only of Catholic France, but also of the two emergent Protestant countries, England and Holland. They refused to accept the Pope's line, or the monopoly of trade that both Spain and Portugal claimed with their colonies. The Dutch who had overtaken the English as skilful shipbuilders and overseas traders were the most successful in their defiance. They had ousted the Portuguese from most of their eastern empire, and had in their turn tried to establish a monopoly. This had brought them into bitter conflict with the English, who claimed at least an equal share.

The Second Dutch War had begun in 1665 with the French in alliance with the Dutch. It had opened with a sea battle off Lowestoft, in which the English fleet of almost one hundred ships, commanded by the Lord High Admiral, James, Duke of York (later to be King James II), defeated a Dutch fleet of equal size, commanded by Jacob van Wassenaer, Lord of Obdam. Eighteen Dutch ships were captured and many more destroyed, including Obdam's flagship, which blew up. The battle was important, too, as a demonstration of the success of the newly developed English method of fighting in a closely-knit line of battle. This enabled ships to give effective support to one another and to bring a concentration of gunfire to bear on the enemy. But the victory was not followed up to make it decisive.

For the rest of that year the English fleet was immobilised in the Thames by the ravages of the Great Plague of London.

In the following spring, the Dutch were again able to assemble a fleet of about one hundred ships, which put to sea under the command of their great admiral, Michiel de Ruyter. The English fleet, now commanded by George Monck, Duke of Albemarle, and Prince Rupert, numbered only eighty. And when false rumours of a French fleet on its way to join de Ruyter were believed, Prince Rupert was ordered down Channel with twenty-five of these ships to oppose it. The Dutch fleet, trying to enter the Channel, was halted by strong south-west winds and anchored off Dunkirk on 11 June. Albemarle, though greatly outnumbered, decided to take advantage of this to throw his whole force against the southern-most Dutch squadron, commanded by Cornelis Tromp.

It was a smart and bold move which might have enabled the English to destroy Tromp's squadron, before the remainder of the Dutch could come to his support. Though he succeeded in inflicting much damage and driving several ships out of action, Albemarle was frustrated by the choppy sea which prevented the ports of the lower tiers of guns being opened. Tromp's ships had cut their cables and

made off towards the friendly shore under their lee. When the shoaling water forced the English to turn away, De Ruyter's fresh ships were able to fall on Albemarle's rear, which was soon in serious trouble.

The *Swiftsure,* commanded by Sir William Berkeley, was surrounded. Her crew fought nobly, but the odds were too great; and when Berkeley collapsed to die from a bullet in his throat, the ship was surrendered.

Another to be heavily beset was Sir John Harman's ship, the *Henry.* Two Dutch fire-ships which crashed into her were hauled clear; a third was sunk by a well-directed broadside. The Dutch Vice-Admiral, Cornelis Evertzen, ranging up alongside, offered quarter to a gallant enemy. 'No, no; it has not come to that yet,' replied the dauntless Harman. The next broadside from the *Henry* killed Evertzen, and in the smoke and confusion the English ship was extricated, limping away to Harwich for repairs.

Through the long summer evening the fight went on. De Ruyter in his journal recorded, 'So that battle between us was a hard-fought one. We fought till 10 o'clock in the evening; then we stopped and thanked God till the 2nd.'

Albemarle would have been justified if he had refused further action. Instead he called his captains on board his flagship and made them a stirring speech in which he said, 'At the worst it will be more honourable to die bravely here on our own element than be made spectacles to the Dutch. To be overcome is the fortune of war; but to fly is the fashion of cowards. So let us teach the world that Englishmen would rather be acquainted with death than fear.' And at daylight the English

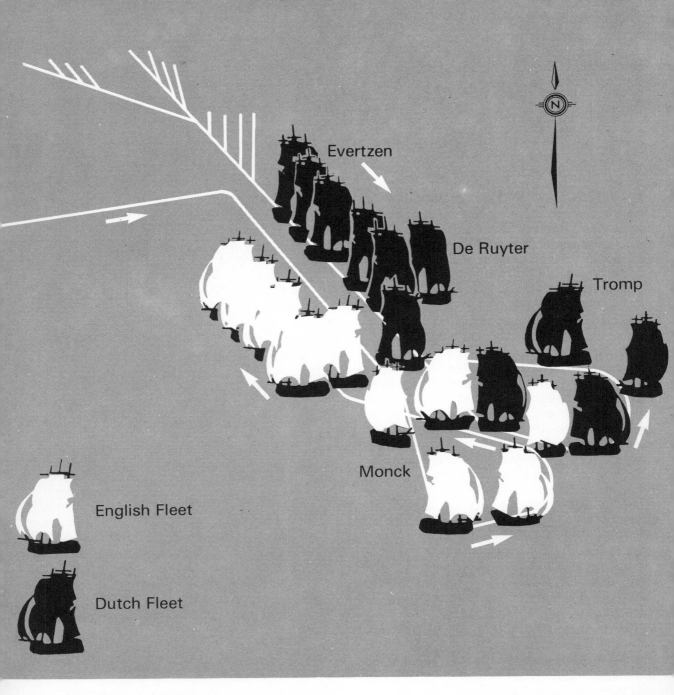

Evertzen

De Ruyter

Tromp

Monck

English Fleet

Dutch Fleet

fleet, now numbering forty-four against the enemy's eighty, reformed their closely-ranged line of battle and sailed valiantly into action.

The two fleets approached one another on opposite courses; the English held the windward position; they were also in a more compact formation. As a French observer in the Dutch flagship, the Comte de Guiche, noted, 'Nothing equals the beautiful order of the English at sea. They bring all their fire to bear on those who draw near them.' Albemarle's van found the Dutch van in some confusion, perhaps missing the guiding hand of the dead Evertzen. In face of the English cannonade they bore away down wind exposing themselves to a damaging, raking fire.

De Ruyter had to follow to reform them;
Tromp, with the best intention, failed to
conform; his squadron became isolated
and suffered considerable damage before
de Ruyter could bring the remainder back
to his support. When a reinforcement of
sixteen fresh ships joined de Ruyter,
Albemarle, at last, conceded that the odds
against him, more than two to one by now,
were too great, and he signalled the retreat.

De Ruyter's journal for that day recorded
that . . . 'the fighting was fierce. Both sides
lost masts and had several topmasts and
yards brought down. About 3 o'clock in the
afternoon my main mast with my flag and
pendant was shot off and my rigging was
greatly damaged . . . Vice-Admirals Van
der Hulst and Schram and Captain den
Haen had to leave the line and make for
home as they were badly damaged . . . Two
Englishmen sank and they did their best
to flee from us . . . We drifted all that night
as there was calm till the 3rd.'

At daylight Albemarle drew up his least
damaged ships, about sixteen in number,
in line to cover the wrecks limping away
towards the Thames estuary. In this he
was successful; but suddenly there occurred a calamity: The *Royal Prince,* finest in
the fleet and flagship of Rear-Admiral
Ayscue, ran aground on the Galloper Shoal.
She was quickly beset and overwhelmed by
a number of the enemy. The English ensign
came fluttering down; Ayscue and all his
men became prisoners of the Dutch.

The *Royal Prince* was never to reach
Holland, however. For away to the south
a cluster of white sails came in sight. At
first both sides thought it was probably the
rumoured French fleet coming to aid their
Dutch allies; then cheers broke out in the
English ships as the newcomers were
identified as Prince Rupert's squadron.
Albemarle turned at bay. De Ruyter was
forced to abandon attempts to refloat the
stranded ship and he ordered it to be burnt.

On the morning of the 14th, the English
fleet, now composed of Rupert's twenty-
five fresh ships and the twenty-five battle-
worn ships of Albemarle's, their crews
cheering and waving their hats defiantly,
sailed gaily into action against de Ruyter's
seventy. They broke through the Dutch
line in gallant style, only to find a further
enemy line beyond.

Sandwiched between the two, they
suffered heavily; but they gave such a good
account of themselves before they were
forced again to retire that de Ruyter broke
off the action. As he recorded in his
Journal, 'the third time the Dutch fell upon
the English fleet from the rear and began
to fight at very close range. Then the
English were put to flight . . . Shortly after,
a heavy fog came up, which was manifestly
the work of the Almighty God. So many
ships were heavily damaged, especially in
their rigging, and many had run short of
powder, so that finally I decided to break
off the engagement and confide the safety
of the Fleet to the hazards of the sea.'

So ended the Four Day's Battle. The
English had lost eight ships destroyed and
seven captured. They had suffered 5,000
casualties and 3,000 were taken prisoner.
The Dutch had lost seven ships and suffered
2,500 casualties. A Dutch victory indeed.
But as the Dutch Grand Pensionary de
Witt, who was present, was to say:

'If the English were beaten, their defeat
did them more honour than all their former
victories. Englishmen may be killed and
English ships burned, but English courage
is invincible!'

The Battle of Quiberon Bay

20 November 1759

It was a wild evening in 1759, with a brutal gale blowing from the west on to a rock-bound shore. On this terrible night a fleet of British sailing ships-of-the-line swept in chase of a similar French force into the Bay of Quiberon on the Biscay coast of Brittany, to fight them while manoeuvring amongst the perilous shallows and breakers. It was seemingly foolhardy to the point of madness; it courted disaster; but peerless skill and seamanship turned it into one of the decisive victories of naval history.

The year 1759 was the third of what was to become known as the Seven Years War to the French and English; as the French and Indian War to the American colonists. The war had started badly for the British; serious defeats had been inflicted in America by the French and their Red Indian allies; a naval reverse in the Mediterranean had lost Minorca; Indian allies of the French had taken Calcutta from the British East India Company. Then the British pulled themselves together, restoring strength and quality to their army and navy.

Robert Clive secured the British possessions in India and ejected the French. Across the Atlantic, Louisburg, the key to Canada, was captured; so was Fort Duquesne, the French outpost on the Ohio, the river link between French Canada in the north and French Louisiana in the south.

But the great climax was to come in 1759. On 1 August the British army played a gallant part on the continent of Europe in the allied victory of Minden. At sea the French Mediterranean Fleet was crippled in the Battle of Lagos on the 18th of the same month; eleven days later Quebec, and with it the whole of Canada, was captured by a combined land and sea force under Wolfe and Saunders.

Since June the French Atlantic Fleet at Brest had been closely blockaded by a fleet under Admiral Sir Edward Hawke. This meant that the French were unable to escort the transports of an invasion force prepared against Ireland. These were similarly locked up in the Morbihan estuary on the north shore of Quiberon Bay where a small detached British squadron kept a constant watch.

The season for wild Atlantic gales out of the west drew on, and on 9 November 1759 one of them forced Hawke's storm-battered ships to run for shelter in Torbay. When the wind relented and swung round to blow from the south, they were quickly under way again and heading back to their station off the black rocks of Ushant. But the same wind allowed the French admiral, the Marquis de Conflans, to lead his fleet of twenty-one ships-of-the-line to sea from Brest; and on the 15th the scouting frigate *Gibraltar*, every sail spread, raced to join Hawke with the news that the French were out.

The British admiral guessed at once that Quiberon Bay and release of the transports would be de Conflans' objective and he determined to follow him with all possible speed. For four baffling days the wind continued dead foul, however, blowing from the south, and it was not until the 19th that at last it shifted to north-westerly. Under a press of towering, snowy sails Hawke's twenty-three battleships could now drive south-eastwards towards Belle Isle, Quiberon's island shelter from the Atlantic rollers.

The small detached squadron under

Commodore Duff, watching the transports in the Morbihan, had been able to ride out the gale under the lee of Belle Isle; but they were now in danger of being trapped by de Conflans. The French fleet had, like Hawke, been delayed by contrary winds. All the same, when the frigate *Vengeance* sailed into the anchorage early on the 20th, signals fluttering to report to Duff that the enemy fleet was bearing down upon him, the situation was perilous enough. At Duff's orders his ships cut their cables, made sail with all haste and steered to escape south of Belle Isle. But the leading French ship, a two-decker of 74 guns, was almost within gun shot of Duff's slowest sailer, the 50-gun *Chatham* when, from the masthead of Duff's flagship, the 50-gun *Rochester,* came the look-out's hail of a second fleet, beyond the French, to the north-west.

Duff realised at once that this must be Hawke in the nick of time to the rescue. Boldly he turned on his pursuers, but de Conflans hastily recalled his ships as he realised that the newcomers were sweeping down on him on the wind to force a fleet action. Hawke, indeed, had signalled 'General Chase', which permitted his ships to press on at their utmost speed without regard to station in any formation. The French admiral made an effort to get his ships into a line of battle; but in the ever increasing westerly gale the leading British ships were coming up fast. He decided that his best plan was to run for the protection of the rock-strewn waters of Quiberon Bay. They were dangerous enough, even for him, in the wild onshore gale that was lashing them into a foam-flecked frenzy, though well-known and charted for his pilots; but much more hazardous for the enemy.

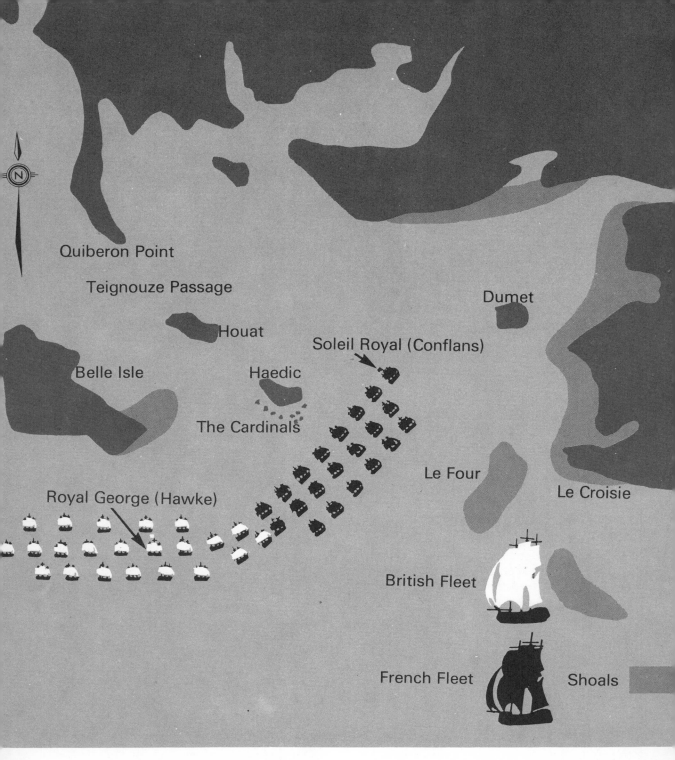

Quiberon Point

Teignouze Passage

Dumet

Houat

Soleil Royal (Conflans)

Belle Isle

Haedic

The Cardinals

Le Four

Le Croisie

Royal George (Hawke)

British Fleet

French Fleet

Shoals

At about two o'clock in the afternoon, the foremost British ships, the *Warspite* (74 guns) and the *Dorsetshire* (70 guns), followed by the *Revenge* (64 guns), *Magnanime* (74 guns), *Torbay* (74 guns), *Montagu* (60 guns), *Resolution* (74 guns), *Swiftsure* (70 guns), and *Defiance* (60 guns) came one after the other into action. On deck, to the bellowed orders of the sailing masters, sailors hauled on braces, sheets and halliards to trim the sails to the whistling wind. Aloft, others out on the yards, were securing thrashing canvas. Down in the smoke-filled gloom of the gun-decks, the remainder served the deafening cannon which leaped viciously back against the rope breechings as they fired, then to be re-loaded and run out till their black muzzles thrust out through the gun ports. It all added up to a scene of apparent confusion; but it was one in which the British seamen, hardened and trained by continuous sea-going in all weathers to keep guard on their harbour-bound enemies, had a clear advantage.

De Conflans led round the Cardinal Rocks into the Bay, hoping his pursuers would not dare to follow. He had under-estimated them. Without hesitation they turned into the leaping turmoil of spray-whipped water, their broadsides thunder-ing out as they overtook the rear French ships. Target for every ship that passed was the *Formidable* (80 guns), flagship of the French Rear-Admiral du Verger. By four o'clock she had been battered to a wreck; more than two hundred of her crew had been killed and now she hauled her flag down to surrender to the *Resolution*.

Even greater disaster overtook the French *Thésée* (70 guns) and *Superbe* (74 guns), both of which sank with nearly all hands, chiefly through keeping open their lower rows of gunports. The seas poured in as the ships heeled under the pressure of the wind. Another ship forced to strike her colours, was the *Héros* (74 guns), but so rough was it that no prize crew could be sent over to her.

By this time the short November day was fading to a dark night of storm. With a lee shore close by, a mortal peril always in those days of clumsy sailing men-of-war,

it was time to call off the chase. Signalling for the fleet to do the same, Hawke's flag-ship, the huge 100-gun three-decker *Royal George,* dropped anchor in the middle of Quiberon Bay. Some of his ships did not take in the signal—not surprising in the wild conditions of that evening—and they spent a hazardous night beating out to sea. All night long distress guns could be heard but no-one could send help in such wild weather.

A gale-swept dawn brought with it an element of comedy. For in the middle of Hawke's ships could be seen at anchor the three-decker *Soleil Royal,* de Conflans' flagship. She hastily cut her cables and tried to get away, only to drift ashore near the town of St. Croisec, where later she was burnt by her own people. The *Essex,* ordered to chase her, grounded on the Four Bank where the French *Héros* had also fetched up. The *Essex* was wrecked and the *Héros* burned.

Other things to be seen as daylight increased, were the British *Resolution* and the French *Juste* (70 guns) both wrecked on shore, while in the mouth of the River Vilaine in the north-east corner of Quiberon Bay, five French ships-of-the-line were hastily getting out guns and stores to lighten themselves and reach sanctuary in the river. The remainder of the French had fled south and taken shelter at Rochefort.

Thus, for the loss of two of his own ships and some fifty men killed and two hundred and fifty wounded, Hawke's fleet had taken or destroyed seven French ships of the line and eliminated others which could never be put to sea again. French sea-power in the Seven Years War was finally eclipsed by this battle, while the reputation of British seamen soared to new heights.

Camperdown

12 October 1797

The little hamlet of Kamperduin on the coast of the Netherlands, near Egmont, some twenty miles south from the Dutch naval port, the Texel, is not even marked on atlases today. But nearly two hundred years ago it was well-known to everyone in Britain as Camperdown, and it is still remembered as the name given to a decisive victory of the Royal Navy.

The year 1797 saw Britain's fortunes in the war against Revolutionary France at a low ebb. Even at sea, though the Revolution had reduced the French Navy to a state of disorder and inefficiency, the Royal Navy had been unable to prevent a French invasion fleet carrying an army to Bantry Bay in Ireland at the previous Christmas. Only the winter storms had ruined the French plan. The British fleet had been forced to abandon the Mediterranean; and, though a Spanish fleet had been soundly beaten off Cape St. Vincent in February, two months later the main British fleet had been swept by the great mutiny of the crews who were demanding long-overdue improvements in their conditions of service. For a whole month the Channel Fleet lay at Spithead out of action.

When the crews returned to their duty as a result of concessions made by the Admiralty, it became the turn of the North Sea Fleet based on Yarmouth and the Nore to revolt. This brought about an even more dangerous situation. Lying in the Texel was a Dutch fleet of some twenty ships-of-the-line. Since French armies had overrun Holland in 1795 and the puppet Batavian Republic had been set up, this fleet had been an enemy ready and waiting for the opportunity to escort a French invasion force to Ireland. And having escaped the worst excesses of the Revolution which had undermined discipline in the French Navy, it was a formidable force. Only the close blockade maintained by the North Sea Fleet had kept it penned in harbour.

In spite of the importance of this duty, the North Sea Fleet, commanded by Admiral Adam Duncan, was treated by the Admiralty as of secondary importance to the Channel Fleet. To it the oldest and least seaworthy ships of the Navy were allocated; even the *Venerable,* the 74-gun fleet flagship, was so leaky that it was a constant labour to keep her afloat. Nevertheless, month after month the blockade had been kept up.

The little armed cutters of the fleet hovered close enough inshore to count the enemy daily in the Texel and watch for any signs of getting under way. Reports were passed to frigates in the offing who in turn signalled to an advanced unit of two line-of-battle ships. Farther out the bulk of the fleet cruised, single ships being sent away as necessary to Yarmouth or the Channel anchorage known as the Downs to make repairs, to take in fresh water and provisions.

Adam Duncan, the 6 foot 4 inches tall Scottish admiral had prevented, by his commanding personality, the infection of mutiny spreading to the crew of his flagship. He had been able to do so in one other of his ships-of-the-line, the 64-gun *Adamant.* Here he had nipped mutiny in the bud when he seized the ringleader by the collar and held him over the side at the end of one extended arm. 'Look at this fellow who dares to deprive me of the command of the fleet,' he cried; a roar of good-natured laughter brought trouble to an end. But Duncan could not be everywhere and at the end of May all the other ships-

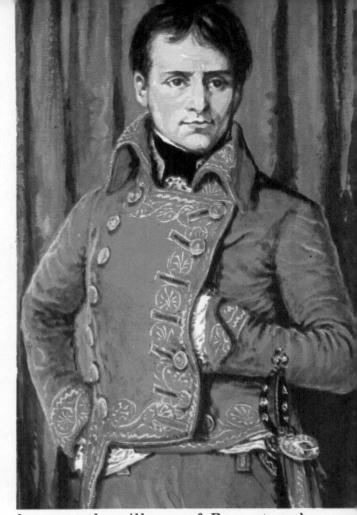

of-the-line had sailed to the Nore to join the mutiny.

Left with only two battleships to face an enemy fleet of nearly a score, he had resorted to bluff. Patrolling in sight of the Texel he busily hoisted flag signals to an imaginary fleet supposed to be below the horizon from Dutch watchers on the shore. Fortunately, the French expedition had not been ready at this time. By the time it was, the mutinies were over and Duncan's ships had returned to him, their crews now eager to show their loyalty and patriotism in battle. Through July and August contrary winds held the Dutch fleet in harbour. Finally plans for the French expedition were abandoned for that year.

In spite of this, early in October, the Dutch admiral, John William de Winter, received orders from the committee at the Hague which managed the naval affairs of the 'Batavian Republic' to put to sea as soon as the wind was favourable and offer battle.

Thus it was that early on the 9th, the lugger *Speculator* arrived under a press of sail off Yarmouth, where Duncan had anchored most of his storm-battered ships a week earlier for repairs, and to give rest to his tired crews. The little scout brought the urgent news that the Dutch were at sea, fifteen ships-of-the-line, five frigates and five brigs. They were being shadowed by the two ships that Duncan had left watching off the Texel, the *Russell* (74 guns) and the *Adamant,* as they steered south-west down the coast of the Netherlands.

The British fleet sailed at once and, early on the 12th, the frigate *Circe,* scouting ahead, signalled the enemy in sight to the south-east, about five miles off shore

between the villages of Egmont and Camperdown. De Winter, who had achieved his rank by reason of his pro-revolutionary views and had never himself commanded a ship, had little confidence in himself or in his unpractised ships' companies. On hearing that Duncan was at sea, he decided to turn for home. At the same time he would try to lay a trap for his enemy. His ships drew less water than the British and so could navigate safely amongst the off-shore shallows.

And there Duncan sighted him at 9 a.m., drawing up his ships into a line of battle on a north-easterly course. The British admiral saw that he had no time to spare for such manoeuvres if he wished to bring the enemy to action before he got amongst the shoals.

Though his own fleet was advancing before the northwesterly wind in two

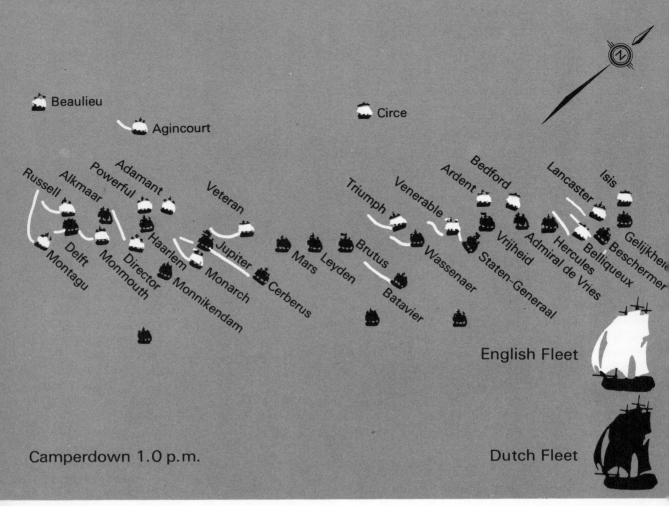

Beaulieu

Agincourt

Circe

Russell
Alkmaar
Powerful
Adamant
Veteran
Triumph
Venerable
Ardent
Bedford
Lancaster
Isis

Montagu
Delft
Monmouth
Director
Haarlem
Monnikendam
Jupiter
Monarch
Cerberus
Mars
Leyden
Brutus
Batavier
Wassenaer
Staten-Generaal
Vrijheid
Admiral de Vries
Hercules
Belliqueux
Beschermer
Gelijkheid

English Fleet

Dutch Fleet

Camperdown 1.0 p.m.

unformed groups, the northern led by his own flagship, the *Venerable,* and the southern by Vice-Admiral Onslow, his second-in-command, in the *Monarch,* he signalled simply for his ships to break through the enemy line and engage them on their lee side, thus getting between them and the land. The two groups steered so as to bring a concentration against the Dutch van and rear leaving the centre at first out of the battle.

The two fleets now clearing for action, where the grim preparations for battle were going forward to the rumble of the great guns as they were run out on their wooden carriages, were about equal in numbers and in the calm courage with which the crews faced the daunting ordeal before them. But there were two things in which the British had an advantage. The arma-ment of their ships included a number of

carronades, short-barrelled cannon firing 68-pound shot which at short range could cause such damage that they were known as 'smashers'. The Dutch had none of these. And in seamanship and gunnery, the two qualities on which victory most depended, the British, continuously at sea in all weathers, were greatly superior to their long harbour-penned opponents.

The first guns to bellow forth were those of the *Jupiter* (74 guns), flagship of the Dutch Rear-Admiral Reyntjes. They were aimed at the *Monarch* leading the southern British group which did not deign to reply, until, passing through the line, she was in position to 'rake', that is to fire lengthwise into, a Dutch ship on either side. Then her broadsides thundered out at the *Jupiter* to port, the *Haarlem* to starboard at point blank range, wreaking fearful damage and casualties.

At this point the 44-gun frigate *Monnikendam* gallantly challenged the 74-gun *Monarch,* drawing on herself that ship's second broadside which crippled her and caused many casualties. The frigate continued to fight as she drifted down the line and only when she was reduced to a total wreck with fifty lying dead and sixty wounded, did she haul down her colours.

Meanwhile the southern British group of nine ships were fighting the five rear ships of the enemy. Such odds were too great to endure for long and within an hour four of them had surrendered; the fifth, the 56-gun *Alkmaar* held out alone for another hour.

Three of Onslow's ships, the *Powerful, Director* and *Veteran,* were now free to sail on up the line to assist the northern group. There, Duncan's flagship *Venerable,* had found herself for a time surrounded by four enemy ships and in danger of being overwhelmed. But help came from the *Lancaster* and *Belliqueux* in the van, as well as from the *Powerful* and *Director.* The fierce and gallant resistance in the van ships of the Dutch fleet was worn down; one after the other they hauled down their flags and their guns fell silent on decks littered with the dead and wounded.

De Winter's flagship *Vrijheid,* where more than 150 had been killed or wounded, could claim never to have lowered her flag as it had been shot away again and again until there were no more left; nor had she a mast left on which to hoist one. All three lay shattered in a tangle of wreckage. There was no resistance, however, when the first lieutenant of the *Director* climbed on board from a boat; the Dutch admiral, the only officer unwounded on deck, then yielded and was rowed over to the *Venerable*. When he offered his sword in surrender, Duncan refused to take it saying, 'I would much rather take a brave man's hand than his sword.'

Two of the Dutch van, the *Beschemer* and Rear-Admiral Storij's flagship, the *Staten-Generaal,* much shattered at the first encounter, drifted out of the fight and later escaped. Five of the Dutch centre, left unopposed as a result of Duncan's concentration on the van and rear, were also led away to safety by Rear-Admiral Bloijs Van Treslong in the *Brutus,* who was later to be court-martialled for his failure to support his chief.

That the remainder fought with traditional Dutch gallantry and surrendered only when all hope of resistance had gone, may be judged from the fact that none of the eleven Dutch ships captured were ever fit to go to sea again. The grievous toll of casualties on either side tells a similar tale – some 800 British and 1200 Dutch.

As a consequence of the battle, the Dutch fleet was eliminated as a fighting force. It never came to sea again before being surrendered two years later, when a British expeditionary force invaded the Netherlands.

Honours were showered on Duncan and his captains, he himself being created Viscount Duncan of Camperdown. His sailors' reward was mainly their share of the prize-money allocated in those days to the captors of enemy ships. It could not compensate the many wounded for the loss of legs or arms or other crippling injuries; but a Patriotic Fund opened by Lloyd's, the great London Insurance agency, on their behalf, raised £52,609 a sum equivalent to many times that figure in today's money.

The Battle of the Nile
1 August 1798

It has been recorded earlier how Britain, standing alone in opposition to a Republican France ambitious to dominate Europe, had reached a low ebb in her fortunes during 1797. For a time she had been defenceless, with the ships of her Channel and North Sea Fleets flying the red flag of mutiny. Then the crews had returned to their duty and wiped out the disgrace in the hard-fought victory of Camperdown. The situation in northern waters was thus restored.

In the Mediterranean, however, no British warship had been seen since the beginning of that year. It had become a French lake, and the brilliant French general, Napoleon Bonaparte, one day to make himself Emperor of the French, dreamed of a career of worldwide conquest. He would take an army to Egypt as a first step on the route to India. A huge expedition with some four hundred transports carrying 36,000 troops was assembled at French Mediterranean ports; in Toulon, a fighting fleet escort of thirteen ships-of-the-line and eight frigates commanded by Vice-Admiral Brueys.

When news of these preparations reached Admiral Lord St. Vincent, commanding the blockading fleet off the coast of Spain, in May 1798, he detached a squadron of three ships-of-the-line and three frigates under his brilliant subordinate, Rear-Admiral Horatio Nelson, to keep a watch on them. This was damaged and scattered by a furious gale, and while Nelson's flagship *Vanguard* was being repaired in Sardinia, the French fleet got under way on 19 May. Between then and 9 June it cruised slowly east and south, picking up the several contingents of troopships from French and Italian ports and finally assembled off Malta. On the next day Malta was assaulted and captured from the Knights of St. John.

Nelson, arriving off Toulon again on 31 May, heard of the French departure; but where they had gone to was a complete mystery. When reinforcements reached him on 7 June, bringing his fleet up to thirteen ships-of-the-line and one smaller ship of 50 guns, he steered for Naples, capital of the one small Mediterranean state still holding out against French aggression. There he was directed on to Malta, only to learn on 22 June that the enemy had quitted Malta, sailing away on a north-west wind that suggested their destination might be Alexandria, the port of Egypt.

Setting off in pursuit, he was off Alexandria on the 28th. His single scout, the brig *Mutine,* was sent in to examine the harbour and returned to report it empty. Distressed and anxious, Nelson turned away to search elsewhere. He had, in fact, overtaken the enemy fleet, all unawares, during a dark and foggy night. It was to cause the fiery little admiral five agonised weeks of bitter frustration, but he put them to good use.

Time and again he gathered his captains together, welding them into his 'band of brothers'. When they finally met the enemy they would know just what he expected of them. On 19 July he was at Syracuse (Sicily) stirring up agents and merchants to provide fresh provisions and water for his fleet as quickly as possible. By the 24th he was off again steering eastward; four days later his old friend Tom Troubridge, captain of the *Culloden* (74 guns), sent in to the Greek port of Koroni for news, and was told that the French fleet had been seen four weeks earlier off the south coast of Crete, steering south-east.

So once again Nelson steered for Alexandria. On 1 August it came into sight. The French flag was flying over the city. The harbour was packed with shipping, but the *Alexander* and *Swiftsure* sent in to get a close look, reported they were nearly all merchantmen and transports with just a few small ships of war. It seemed that Nelson's prey, the French fleet, had given him the slip, after all the long weary weeks of pursuit.

But then, at 1 p.m., from the *Zealous*, sent to scout to the eastward, came the electrifying signal – seventeen enemy ships of war at anchor in Aboukir Bay, a dozen miles along the coast. Spreading every available sail, Nelson hurried eastward on the wings of a brisk breeze from the north-northwest. By 3 p.m., he could see Brueys' battle ships anchored in a line running roughly north to south. The long chase was over. To the *Vanguard*'s masthead sped the flag signal for 'Prepare for Battle'.

In every ship the boatswain's whistles shrilled as the order was passed through the various decks. It was followed by the drumming of hundreds of bare feet as the sailors ran to their stations to start the often-practised task of clearing ship for action. The gunports were opened, the guns unlashed, loaded and run out with a thunderous rumble. The decks were sanded lest they should become slippery with blood later. The youngest of the ship's company, the boys called powder-monkeys, earned their nickname as they carried cartridges from the magazines to the guns. And in the cockpit, deep down near the ship's bottom, the surgeon and his assistants prepared the tools of their craft.

The French fleet, thirteen of the line and four frigates, had arrived at Alexandria on

Right:
Nelson realised that Brueys had miscalculated his defensive position in Aboukir Bay. For where there was room for a French ship to swing round on her anchor, there must also be room for a British ship to sail between it and the shoals.

1 July, three days after Nelson's first inspection of the port. Napoleon had at once landed his troops and seized the city. On the 8th, finding the harbour too crowded, Brueys had moved his fighting ships to Aboukir Bay. There he had anchored them in a line as close as possible and parallel to the shallows which extended out from the western horn of the bay, enclosing little Aboukir Island. This, in fact, left a certain area of moderately deep water between the ships and the shoal, in which Brueys had anchored his four frigates. He evidently thought, however, that his position was such that an enemy would have to attack him only from seaward. With extra men brought on board his battleships from his frigates and gunboats and with none required for handling sails, he felt that this gave him the advantage.

But he was up against the greatest seaman of his age. As Nelson got a full view of the situation it was at once clear to him that where there was room for a French ship to swing round on her anchor, there must be room for his own to sail between them and the shoals. Indeed, this was one of the possible situations he had discussed with his captains. They all knew just what to do. When Nelson signalled that he intended to attack the enemy's van and centre, they knew that the leading ships must try to get between the enemy and the shore. Then as the others came up and engaged from seaward, the head of the enemy line would be caught between two fires. Long before their ships in the rear could come to their rescue, the French van and centre would be destroyed.

And nobly Nelson's captains followed his plan. It was just 6.20 p.m., with the sun about to set behind the desert sands, when the two leading French ships, *Guerrier* and *Conquérant,* opened fire on the *Goliath,* leading the British line and the *Zealous* close astern of her.

The two British ships held their fire until, as they passed close ahead of the *Guerrier,* they were able to rake that unfortunate ship from end to end with a full port broadside each. The *Goliath,* having anchored abreast the *Conquérant,* poured her port broadsides into her, while to starboard she attacked the frigate *Sérieux.*

The *Zealous* had anchored on the port bow of the *Guerrier* which she continued to rake. Five minutes after the action opened and just as the sun set, the *Guerrier's* foremast crashed down to the roaring cheers of the leading British crews.

The *Orion* was the next to round the *Guerrier.* She sailed down the French line and having dismasted and wrecked the *Sérieux* as she passed, anchored on the port side of the *Peuple Souverain* and settled down to a steady exchange of broadsides.

Two other ships broke through to the inshore side of the French line, *Audacious* and *Theseus.* The *Audacious* placed herself only fifty yards off the bow of the *Conquérant* which was now beset by two ships each as large as herself. The *Theseus* sailed on to anchor abreast the *Spartiate* on the opposite side of which Nelson's *Vanguard* stationed herself.

Soon after his flagship got into action, Nelson was wounded, his forehead being slashed and a flap of flesh falling over his one good eye. (He had lost the sight of the other in action some years before.) In terrible pain he was carried below to the cockpit for treatment. But when the surgeon left what he was doing and came to attend to him he refused to accept any

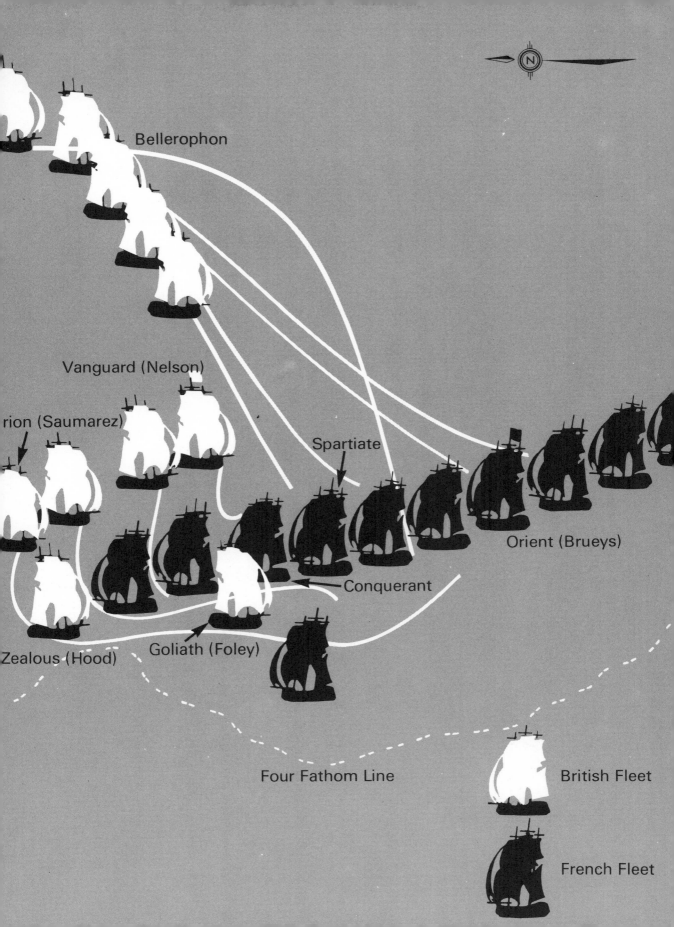

Bellerophon

Vanguard (Nelson)

rion (Saumarez)

Spartiate

Conquerant

Orient (Brueys)

Zealous (Hood)

Goliath (Foley)

Four Fathom Line

British Fleet

French Fleet

preference. 'No', he said, 'I will take my
turn with my brave fellows.' Fortunately
the wound proved more painful than
dangerous and Nelson recovered.

By 7 p.m. the *Minotaur* and *Defence* had
sailed into the fight to anchor abreast the
Aquilon and the *Peuple Souverain.* It was
dark by now. Eight British ships were
engaging five French. This was the battle-
winning concentration that Nelson had
planned.

The remainder of the British battleships
were meanwhile slanting down to pick
their opponents. For the next in the line,
the *Bellerophon* (the *Billy-Ruffian* to her
sailors), this turned out to be the huge,
three-decker, 120-gun French flagship the
Orient. It was terrible odds for the 74-gun
British ship which soon began to suffer
heavily. By 8 p.m., totally dismasted, she
was drifting away out of action.

Another ship which had cut or parted
her cable and was dropping down wind was
the *Peuple Souverain.* The *Majestic* and
Leander were more evenly matched than
the *Bellerophon.* The former engaged the
Tonnant, while the *Leander* skilfully
anchored herself so that with her starboard
guns she could rake the *Aquilon* and with
her port broadside the *Franklin.*

Now the *Swiftsure* arrived to take the
place of the *Bellerophon;* the *Alexander*
also anchored where she could engage the
Orient. In action now were all Nelson's
ships except one, Troubridge's *Culloden*
which, cutting too closely round Aboukir
Island had gone firmly aground on the
shoal. There she was to remain throughout
the battle, to the impotent fury of all her
crew.

While the five rear ships of the French
line lay idle, unable to join the battle, the
rest, though fighting bravely against great
odds, were being overwhelmed. By 9.30 p.m.
the *Guerrier*, *Conquérant*, *Spartiate*,
Aquilon and *Franklin* had been battered
into surrender. The *Peuple Souverain* had
re-anchored but had been so shattered that
she played little further part. It was on
Admiral Brueys' flagship, *Orient,* that
attention now centred.

After disabling the *Bellerophon,* she had
been assailed by the *Swiftsure* and the
Alexander. Earlier in the battle the admiral
had been almost cut in two by a roundshot.
As gentle hands tried to carry him below,
he summoned up strength to say 'Let me
be. A French admiral dies on his own
quarterdeck.' Under the concentrated fire
of the two British 74's, the *Orient* had been
reduced to a shambles.

But now that most dreaded thing in the
days of wooden ships and tarred rope—
fire—was seen to break out on her. As the
Swiftsure concentrated her gunfire on the
flames, they spread along the deck and
leaped up the rigging. The night was
hideously lit by them. Soon the whole ship
was ablaze. At about 10 p.m. the expected
occurred; the great ship blew up in one
great shattering explosion. The thunder of
battle died away as the awe-struck sailors
on both sides looked on, shocked and still.

From the British ships, boats were
launched and picked up about seventy of
the crew. The Chief of Staff, Rear-Admiral
Ganteaume, and a few others escaped by a
seeming miracle to a French brig. All the
rest were killed.

After a while the gunfire broke out again.
But the battle was nearly over. By midnight
the seven ships ahead of the *Tonnant* had
all surrendered or been destroyed. The
Tonnant alone continued defiant, putting

up a magnificent defence under her gallant Captain Dupetit-Thouars. Hideously mangled by several wounds, he stayed on deck propped up in a tub to direct the fight until he died. Not until late the following morning did the *Tonnant* finally strike her tricolour flag.

Meanwhile the ships in the rear of the French line were trying to escape. The *Heureux, Mercure* and *Timoléon* ran aground on the nearby shoals where they were soon forced to surrender. Only two of the French ships of the line, the *Guillaume Tell* and *Généreux,* succeeded in beating out to sea and escaping accompanied by two frigates.

Thus in one night of battle Nelson's tactical genius had eliminated French sea power in the Mediterranean and restored that of Britain. Napoleon's Army of Egypt was cut off from its base. Though it conquered Egypt, it could go neither forward to further conquests nor back to France. Its general abandoned it and was forced to sneak home in a little ship risking capture by the Royal Navy. His plans of world conquest had been shattered by the cannonades of Aboukir Bay. Horatio Nelson, created Baron Nelson of the Nile, was heaped with honours. He had seven more years of life before dying at the height of his glory in the Battle of Trafalgar.

Trafalgar

21 October 1805

FAMOUS SEA BATTLES

The long war between Britain and France came to a temporary halt with the Peace of Amiens in March 1802. It was to be only a breathing space, because neither side had been able to force a decision on the other. Britain remained supreme at sea; France, under Napoleon Bonaparte, soon to be made Emperor of the French, was dominant in Europe. Each mistrusted the other; and when it was discovered that Napoleonic ambitions with regard to Egypt and the East were as firm as ever, Britain refused to evacuate Malta as the Peace Treaty demanded. So, in May 1803, war broke out again.

Napoleon's immediate aim was to eliminate Britain as a power to be reckoned with. To do this he had to throw his incomparable Grand Army, mustered and waiting at Boulogne, across the Channel. There his soldiers would smash the feeble opposition of the islanders' small army and march victoriously to London. There was only one unavoidable difficulty to be overcome. The Royal Navy's domination of the waters of the Channel must be broken.

Napoleon, the world's greatest soldier as he was, had a limited understanding of naval matters. He did not realise that to achieve that aim, the British fleet must be met and decisively defeated in pitched battle. He thought that some ingenious plan would avoid the necessity.

His various naval squadrons, divided between the ports of Brest in Brittany, Rochefort in the Bay of Biscay, Ferrol in Northern Spain and Toulon in the Mediterranean, and the fleet of his Spanish allies at Cadiz, were to break out through the blockade established by the Royal Navy, sail across the Atlantic to the West Indies and return as one huge fleet. Sweeping aside any opposition met at the entrance to the Channel, they would sail on to give the necessary protection to the vast assembly of troop-carrying barges in the French Channel ports as they ferried the Grand Army across.

Earlier, we have seen Philip II of Spain's Invincible Armada meet disaster attempting similar strategy. Napoleon's fleet was to be even further from achieving it. Even if the several French squadrons managed to give the Royal Navy the slip and disappear into the vastness of the ocean, the blockading squadrons they had evaded had standing orders to fall back on the Western Squadron in the Channel Approaches. So the French and Spanish Fleet would have to face a British one at least as large when it returned across the Atlantic.

But Bonaparte's plan went wrong from the start. His Brest squadron, and the French and Spanish ships at Ferrol failed to evade the blockade and, forbidden to accept battle, they put back into harbour.

The Toulon squadron under Admiral Villeneuve, on the other hand, which could only be kept under watch by one or two scouting frigates from Admiral Nelson's Mediterranean squadron based in Sardinia, did manage to get clear away. Hurrying through the Straits of Gibraltar on a lucky easterly wind, Villeneuve picked up the five Spanish ships-of-the-line which were lying ready at Cadiz and sailed on across the Atlantic to the French West Indian island of Martinique.

Lack of knowledge of Villeneuve's course at first, and then a long period of contrary winds, put Nelson a full month behind. But when he knew where Villeneuve was heading, he set off in chase with such energy that he gained ten days on passage.

Villeneuve, with Nelson now so close on his heels, could not wait any longer for the Brest squadron. Back across the Atlantic he hurried, having achieved almost nothing. Sending a fast despatch brig off to England with this important news, Nelson also headed back, making for Gibraltar in case Villeneuve tried to re-enter the Mediterranean. Off the north-west corner of Spain the French and Spanish ships were intercepted by a British squadron and after a confused fight amidst banks of fog, in which two Spanish ships were captured, Villeneuve took shelter in Vigo Bay.

So Napoleon's Grand Design had collapsed leaving the French and Spanish fleet as divided as ever. Nelson's task as Commander-in-Chief, Mediterranean, was over for the time being. He was ordered home with his flagship, the *Victory*. His weary body which had not set foot on shore for more than two years, was to rest and recuperate ready for the great and final climax of his life which he felt to be approaching.

Meanwhile Villeneuve had briefly evaded the blockade and sailed from Vigo to join the French and Spanish squadrons at Ferrol. His fleet now totalled twenty-nine ships-of-the-line. His impatient Emperor, waiting at Boulogne with his armies, spurred him on to go north to join the Brest squadron. Alternatively he was to go south to Cadiz in preparation to take the combined French and Spanish fleet into the Mediterranean. For Bonaparte had at last seen the flaws in his invasion plans, and was preparing to take his Grand Army eastward to attack the Austrians and Prussians, the allies of England.

Fourteen of Villeneuve's ships had been

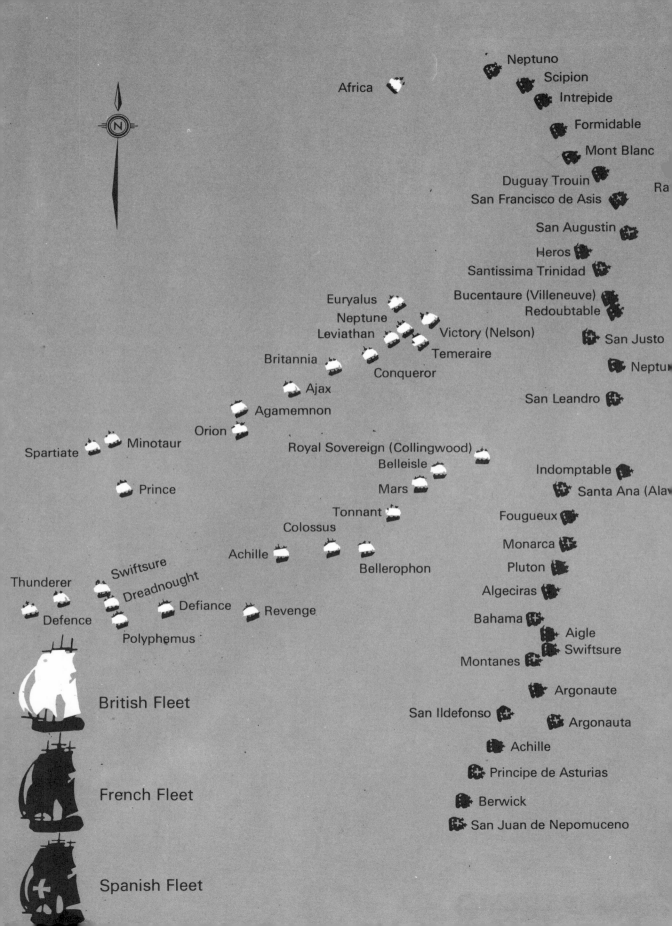

Africa

Neptuno
Scipion
Intrepide
Formidable
Mont Blanc
Duguay Trouin
San Francisco de Asis
Ra
San Augustin
Heros
Santissima Trinidad
Euryalus
Neptune
Bucentaure (Villeneuve)
Leviathan
Redoubtable
Victory (Nelson)
Britannia
Temeraire
San Justo
Conqueror
Ajax
Neptu
Agamemnon
San Leandro
Orion
Royal Sovereign (Collingwood)
Spartiate
Minotaur
Belleisle
Indomptable
Prince
Mars
Santa Ana (Ala
Tonnant
Fougueux
Colossus
Monarca
Achille
Pluton
Swiftsure
Bellerophon
Algeciras
Thunderer
Dreadnought
Bahama
Aigle
Defence
Defiance
Swiftsure
Polyphemus
Revenge
Montanes
Argonaute
San Ildefonso
Argonauta
Achille
Principe de Asturias
Berwick
San Juan de Nepomuceno

British Fleet

French Fleet

Spanish Fleet

Left:
Nelson's plan was to bear down on the enemy in such a way that his whole fleet would concentrate on the rear two-thirds of the enemy's line. If this were done, he was sure that victory would have been achieved before the enemy's van ships could get back to assist the centre and rear.

harbour-bound since the war began and Villeneuve had no confidence in being able to face the hardened, highly-trained ships of the Western Squadron. So when at last the opportunity came to put out on 13 August 1805, he took advantage of his alternative orders and turned south.

Off Cadiz the little blockade squadron of three ships-of-the-line under Vice-Admiral Cuthbert Collingwood could do nothing but watch him file into the harbour. But once he was in, reinforcements were sent to join Collingwood. The trap door was slammed shut. Villeneuve could only escape by accepting a fight with the British fleet.

The combined French and Spanish fleets now numbered thirty-three ships-of-the-line against twenty-seven British, but Villeneuve and his Staff knew all too well that, unpractised and long harbour-bound as most of them were, they were no match for their enemies who had kept the seas unceasingly through every kind of foul weather since the war began. They were still less anxious to challenge them when the news reached the Combined Fleet that the heroic Nelson had arrived in the *Victory* to take over the command.

But Villeneuve found himself on the horns of a dilemma. His dread master, the Emperor, had given him firm orders to get to sea and take his fleet to the Mediterranean. In case he should delay, his successor, Admiral Rosily, was posting to Cadiz and would arrive in a few days. Villeneuve had the choice between disgrace and ruin on the one hand; a desperate fight in which he had no faith in winning on the other.

And so, on 19 October the Combined Fleet began to put to sea. Nelson had with-

drawn some 50 miles to seaward so as not to discourage his opponent from coming out. But a chain of frigates kept him informed of every move.

It was not until the morning of the 20th that the whole of the Combined Fleet got out under the light and fickle breezes round the harbour mouth. Then Villeneuve steered westward out into the Atlantic to gain an offing which would allow him to clear the shoals off Cape Trafalgar and make for the Straits of Gibraltar. Nelson, with his fleet in cruising order of two columns, sailing abreast of each other, steered to intercept: twelve ships in the column following the *Victory,* fifteen in that led by Collingwood's flagship, *Royal Sovereign.*

It was in this formation when, at dawn, on the 21st the Combined Fleet came in sight, a mass of white sails covering the eastern horizon. The opportunity had come for Nelson to try out his long-pondered plan to bring about a really decisive victory. This had never yet been achieved between two sailing fleets on the high seas.

The accepted formation in which such a fleet should fight was the 'single-line ahead': ships following one another in a single line. When two such columns met and cannonaded each other, even the least well-fought side would usually be able to inflict enough damage to prevent the victor from capturing or destroying more than one or two of the opposition.

The problem was how to concentrate one's whole force against an inferior part of the enemy's and overwhelm it before the remainder could come to its aid. Nelson's plan had two main points. Firstly, to avoid spending valuable time changing from his cruising disposition to a single battle line,

'the order of sailing would be the order of battle.' Secondly, the columns of the 'order of sailing' would bear down on the enemy in such a way that the whole fleet would concentrate on the rear two-thirds of the enemy's line, with ships thrusting through to engage the enemy from both sides. If this were done he was sure that victory would have been achieved before the enemy's van ships could get back to assist the centre and rear.

Perhaps more important than the plan itself was Nelson's reliance upon his captains – his 'band of brothers' – carrying out his ideas without any complicated signalling. He had explained it all to them personally in a way no previous admiral had done. He relied, too, upon the superior seamanship and fighting quality of his hardened British 'tars' who could fire two broadsides for every one of the enemy's. All this was what was to be known as 'The Nelson Touch'.

Now all that Nelson needed to do to set his fleet sailing into battle was to signal for the order of sailing to be reformed on a course roughly for the centre of the enemy line. In the light westerly airs blowing, the *Victory* and the *Royal Sovereign* swung ponderously round. Behind them, one by one, followed the others of their respective lines. It would take the whole forenoon to cover the distance between the two fleets at the best speed they could make in the faint prevailing wind. Plenty of time for the crew to have a meal. Then at the gruff call of the drums beating to quarters, the ships would be cleared for action.

Down would come the portable bulkheads forming the walls of the cabins, even those of the 'great cabins' of captains and admirals, to clear the gundecks of obstruction; sand would be liberally strewn to give the sailors' bare feet a firm grip on decks made slippery by blood; the youngest members of the crew, the 'powder-monkeys', would bring up stocks of powder-filled cartridges from the magazines to the guns; down in the cockpit the surgeons would prepare the grim tools of their trade to deal with casualties. Finally the gunports would be opened and with a sound of thunder the great guns themselves on their wooden carriages would be run out.

In the Combined Fleet, similar preparations were going on. Early in the morning Villeneuve saw that he could not avoid battle. To keep a line of retreat open to Cadiz he reversed course to the northward. His unpractised ships were not in a strict line but formed a crescent with the centre to leeward of the van and rear; some had fallen even further to leeward.

As the forenoon crept by, the two British lines advanced majestically, led by their respective flagships. In the *Victory* the little admiral, so revered by his men, indeed by all his countrymen, went the rounds, speaking words of encouragement during the agonising wait for the shock of battle to begin. A little earlier he had been found by his signal officer, Lieutenant Pasco, on his knees penning his immortal prayer before battle. 'May the great God whom I worship grant to my Country, and for the benefit of Europe in general, a great and glorious Victory; and may no misconduct in anyone tarnish it; and may humanity after victory be the predominant feature in the British fleet. For myself, individually, I commit my life to Him who made me, and may His blessing light upon my endeavours for serving my Country faithfully. To Him I resign myself. Amen, Amen, Amen.'

Now there was little more for him to do. But his sense of glory and of the dramatic urged him to make one last signal of encouragement to his men. To the mast-head sped a succession of three-flag groups which were repeated through the fleet. Their meaning as they were decoded was passed through the waiting gundecks: 'England Expects That Every Man Will Do His Duty.' It was greeted everywhere with roars of cheers.

Pacing the *Victory*'s quarter deck with his Flag Captain, Thomas Hardy, Nelson was begged by him and others to change out of the conspicuous, star-decorated coat he was wearing so as not to draw the enemy's small-arm fire on himself–but in vain.

Of the two British flagships, Colling-wood's *Royal Sovereign* had been the nearer of the two to the enemy, and would come under enemy fire first at about noon. She was steered to pass between the huge 112-gun Spanish *Santa Ana,* sixteenth from the enemy's rear–and the French 74-gun *Fougueux* next in line astern of her. Before she could do so, however, she had to put up with a punishing raking fire from both of them without being able to make any effective reply.

This, indeed, was the case with every British ship coming into action on this day; but it was a risk Nelson had deliberately accepted to achieve his plan. To keep down the casualties the sailors were ordered to lie prone on the deck until the time came to man their own broadside guns.

Their turn came at last: as the *Royal Sovereign*'s bow slid between the two enemy ships, her starboard broadside hurled destruction on the *Fougueux,* her port on the towering *Santa Ana* where, at

one blow, fourteen guns were dismounted, four hundred men killed or wounded.

Collingwood's flagship then ranged up alongside the Spaniard and the two ships exchanged broadsides at point blank range. Casualties and damage on either side were heavy; but the *Santa Ana* was utterly shattered by the higher rate of fire of the experienced British gunners.

Meanwhile the rest of Collingwood's squadron, *Belleisle, Mars, Colossus, Tonnant, Bellerophon, Achille, Poly-phemus, Revenge, Dreadnought, Swiftsure, Prince, Defence, Thunderer* and *Defiance,* which during the long approach had spread out to starboard to cover the whole of the enemy's rear, had been facing similar experiences. Each had to submit to raking broadsides before giving the shattering reply of their own.

As masts and rigging tumbled in tangled masses and thick gun smoke obscured the scene, the battle became a confused mêlée. Both sides fought with valour; but the superior seamanship and gunnery of the British crews were bound to prevail.

Meanwhile the *Victory,* with every sail her masts would bear spread to catch the light breeze from the west, had also gone into action shortly after the *Royal Sovereign.* Nelson had ordered Captain Hardy to take her under the stern of Villeneuve's flagship, the *Bucentaure.* As she ploughed slowly forward she was swept by a storm of fire from the *Bucentaure* and the *Redoutable* next astern.

Captain Lucas of the *Redoutable,* seeing Nelson's intention, closed up on the flag-ship. And as the *Victory*'s port guns smashed the *Bucentaure*'s stern, to hurl death and destruction the whole length of the French flagship's decks, her starboard

Right:
A. W. Devis went on board the *Victory* on her return to Portsmouth to interview witnesses and make sketches for his famous painting, *The Death of Nelson.* This illustration is taken from that painting.

bow crashed into the *Redoutable,* and the two ships became locked together side by side. The remainder of the *Victory*'s line, *Téméraire, Neptune, Britannia, Leviathan, Conqueror, Agamemnon, Ajax, Orion, Minotaur* and *Spartiate,* crowding close behind her, picked out other opponents in the enemy's centre. As in Nelson's plan, the ten leading ships of the Combined Fleet were left out of the battle for the time being. So their centre and rear were under attack by a superior number of British ships.

Though only a 74-gun, two-decked ship, the *Redoutable* was no mean foe for the British flagship. For Captain Lucas had specially trained his men for such a situation. Each had been practised in boarding tactics. In the tops, musketeer marksmen picked off men on the enemy's upper deck and hurled grenades amongst them. As soon as the ships swung together, the lower tier of gunports was slammed shut and the gun crews came up armed with muskets to take their stations in the rigging and on the poop and forecastle.

Conspicuous targets for their fire were the British Commander-in-Chief and his flag captain, as they calmly paced the *Victory*'s quarter-deck together. And it was a musketeer in the *Redoutable*'s mizen top who delivered the most notable individual blow in the great battle by shooting Nelson down. The mortally wounded admiral was carried down to the cockpit and the surgeon's attention.

Captain Lucas' efforts to take the *Victory* by boarding were repulsed, however, and when the next ship in the *Victory*'s line, the fighting *Téméraire,* worked her way into position to fire into the *Redoutable,* the French ship was silenced by a single fearful broadside which killed or wounded more than two hundred of her crew. With his ship sinking under him, Lucas ordered her flag to be struck.

Victory and *Téméraire* had been closely followed through the same gap in the enemy's line by the *Neptune, Leviathan* and *Conqueror*. Each had added the fire of their broadsides to the destruction of the *Bucentaure* as they passed through. Then they went on to reduce the huge Spanish 4-decker, the *Santissima Trinidad,* to a tangled wreck.

The battle had, in fact, resolved itself into two confused, smoke-shrouded mêlées one round the *Victory, Bucentaure* and *Santissima Trinidad,* the other round the *Royal Sovereign* and the *Santa Ana.*

In the *Victory*'s cockpit, Nelson lay dying.

The leading ten ships of the Franco-Spanish line under Rear-Admiral Dumanoir, had in the meantime sailed steadily on, ignoring Villeneuve's signals to come back to his assistance. Not until some two hours after the battle began did Dumanoir give orders to tack and reverse course.

In the faint breeze this took as much as an hour to achieve, even with the aid of ships' boats launched to tow the bows round. Even then only two of his ships, the French *Intrépide* and the Spanish *Neptune* steered for the centre of the battle. The remainder either sailed away to Cadiz or followed Dumanoir as he steered down the windward side of the battle, perhaps intending to threaten the rear. But they were met by the last of Nelson's division, *Minotaur* and *Spartiate,* joined later by the *Thunderer* from Collingwood's division.

So damaged in the ensuing gun battle were Dumanoir's ships that he sailed on southwards, taking them out of the action

altogether. By this time, out of twenty French and Spanish ships remaining on the field of battle, seventeen were dismasted wrecks, thirteen of them in possession of British prize crews, and one blazing furiously, the French *Achille*.

Down below where Nelson lay dying, Hardy brought him the news. 'That is well,' Nelson replied, 'but I had bargained for twenty.' Then with great earnestness he said, 'Anchor, Hardy, anchor.' For he had correctly foreseen that a great storm was approaching.

At his beloved admiral's request Hardy knelt beside him and kissed him on the cheek and on the forehead. 'Now I am satisfied. Thank God I have done my duty,' Nelson murmured. And finally, 'God Bless you Hardy.' In the log of the *Victory* the final act of his life is tersely recorded: 'Partial firing continued until 4.30 p.m. when a victory having been reported to the Right Honourable Lord Viscount Nelson, he then died of his wound.'

At the end of the day, as Nelson had expected, nineteen of the enemy had been taken, and one, the *Achille* destroyed by

fire. In the furious storm which followed, the British ships saved themselves by anchoring, by being taken in tow by frigates or, where masts were still standing, by beating to seaward. But it was impossible to save many of the shattered prizes and, in the end, only four were got into Gibraltar. Dumanoir's four ships were also caught and captured as they tried to escape into Rochefort.

So ended the most complete and decisive sea victory of the age of sail. Three enemy admirals, including Villeneuve himself, were brought to England as prisoners of war. In London, a sorrowing people watched as Nelson's body was brought up the river from Greenwich and buried in St. Paul's Cathedral.

The Napoleonic Wars were to continue for another ten years. On land Napoleon was to win great battles. But he was ultimately to be defeated by two things—the stubborn resistance of the huge population of the Russian empire and the absolute domination of the seas by Britain, won in this case by the decisive Battle of Trafalgar.

The Battle of
the Yellow Sea

10 August 1904

Until the latter half of the nineteenth century the two great oriental nations, China and Japan, had kept themselves aloof from the rest of the world. Then the western nations of Europe and America had come demanding that they should enter into normal relations and allow an exchange of trade. It had taken war or the threat of war to persuade them.

While the Chinese retained their ancient, mainly agricultural, way of life, the Japanese had set out, with boundless energy, to copy the technical skills of the westerners, and they armed themselves with similar weapons. By 1904 they had acquired a large modern army and navy and had joined the company of 'Great Powers', who were jealously competing to obtain the greatest influence over the technically backward Chinese Empire. In doing so the Japanese had clashed with the Russians. Each sought to establish control over Manchuria and Korea.

Negotiations for a compromise solution dragged on, and Japanese patience finally ran out. In the early hours of 9 February 1904, the outbreak of war was signalled by the surprise attack by Japanese torpedo boats on the Russian eastern fleet in the anchorage outside Port Arthur–their naval base at the tip of the Kwantung Peninsula. In spite of the complete surprise achieved, only three torpedo hits were scored. Two Russian battleships and one cruiser were damaged; but none sank and all were got into harbour for repairs.

The war that followed was primarily a land campaign in which Japanese armies, landed at Chemulpo on the west coast of Korea, fought to drive the Russians out of Manchuria and, finally, capture Port Arthur. The success of this campaign depended on the Japanese keeping the Yellow Sea open to their troop convoys. The main task of the Japanese fleet under Admiral Togo, therefore, was to keep the Russians blockaded in Port Arthur; or, if they should manage to break out, to engage and defeat them.

For the next six months, the blockade was maintained chiefly by the use of minefields. When the Russians did emerge to challenge Togo's fleet, the *Petropavlovsk,* flagship of the Russian Commander-in-Chief, Makaroff, blew up on a mine and sank, taking the admiral with her. A second battleship was damaged by another mine, and the fleet returned to harbour.

The Japanese also had their losses during this period. Two of their battleships, the *Hatsuse* and *Yashima* were sunk by a Russian minefield; the light cruiser *Yoshino* by collision.

By July the three Russian battleships damaged by the Japanese torpedo attack, had been repaired, giving them a superiority of two in this class. The Japanese had more cruisers, and two of the most powerful took the place of the two lost battleships in the line. The Japanese were very nervous of a Russian sortie and had held up the convoys due to carry large reinforcements to their armies. On the other hand the new Russian commander, Admiral Vitgeft, lacked confidence in the efficiency of his ships so long penned in harbour. He refused to agree with the proposals made by his superior, the Viceroy, that he should go out and fight.

But then at the end of July there had come a direct order from the Tsar. Reluctantly the Russian fleet prepared for sea, and as far as possible, in the absence of tactical training or target practice, for

battle. The gloomy Vitgeft saying good-bye to his friends foretold that 'We shall meet in another world.'

On the morning of 10 August the fleet weighed anchor and steamed out to sea. There they formed up with the six battleships, *Tzesarevitch* (fleet flagship), *Retvizan, Pobieda, Peresviet* (flagship of Rear-Admiral Prince Ukhtomski), *Sevastopol, Poltava* and three cruisers, in one long line. The eight destroyers with a light cruiser and a hospital ship were stationed on the landward side. After steering at first towards the west, no doubt to deceive the Japanese, Vitgeft finally led off in a south-easterly direction.

Outside, Togo was waiting. His main line (1st Division) was composed of the battleships *Mikasa* (flagship), *Asahi, Fuji* and *Shikishima,* and the armoured cruisers *Kasuga* and *Nisshin*. A 3rd Division under Rear-Admiral Dewa, composed of two armoured and three light cruisers, was in company; a 6th Division of old cruisers joined up later and took station five miles astern of the 1st. In the battle about to begin, however, it was to be shown that it was only the big 12-inch guns of the battleships—the 'capital ships'—that really mattered. Togo was thus fighting at odds of four capital ships against the six Russian.

While waiting for his forces to concentrate, he made no determined effort to engage the Russians. He steamed to and fro across the line of advance of the enemy. Vitgeft turned this way and that, trying to get past. If he succeeded he would have a clear line of retreat to the other Russian naval base in the north, Vladivostok, where he could join up with the three large cruisers and force of torpedo boats stationed there.

Let us look at the problem facing Togo. He was reasonably confident that his well-trained fleet was more than a match for the ill-led, unpractised Russians. If he closed in to engage at a decisive range, he would almost certainly win. But in the process his fleet might suffer losses, or such damage as to put it out of action for a long time, and he dared not risk this. His fleet was Japan's only one; while the Russians had a second fleet on the other side of the world in the Baltic, which was being prepared to steam to the Orient. He decided, therefore, that he must rely upon his superior gunnery and fight at long range. Either he would drive the Russians back to Port Arthur or pick off their ships one by one during the long voyage to Vladivostok.

Not until 1 p.m. did the big guns thunder out. The range was seven miles, almost their limit. Nevertheless, unexpectedly it was the Russians who drew first blood as two 12-inch shells smashed into the *Mikasa* causing heavy damage and casualties. It was some time before the Japanese scored with hits on the *Tzesarevitch* and the *Retvizan*. Then Togo made a false move as a result of which Vitgeft slipped past. Togo found himself having to chase the Russians. The head of his line was exposed to a concentration of Russian fire. Both the *Mikasa* and the *Asahi,* next in the line, were hit.

The Russian maximum sustained speed was about fourteen knots. The Japanese could keep up fifteen. Togo decided that he would turn away until out of range. Then, steering parallel to the enemy, he could gradually draw up abreast of them before turning back to resume the gun battle.

It was 3 o'clock when Togo turned away. When he resumed his parallel course he found himself over-taking only very slowly

at first. But at last luck came his way. The *Poltava* had been lagging behind the remainder of the Russians; Vitgeft had to reduce speed to stay with her. This brought the Japanese up abreast the Russian line and at 5.35 Togo turned inwards again and renewed the cannonade. Vitgeft had to press on at his top speed to prevent Togo cutting across ahead of him. The *Poltava,* one of whose engines had finally broken down, was left to her fate.

And now, against all expectations, the Russian gunnery achieved startling success. The *Mikasa* was repeatedly hit and had her after turret put out of action. In the *Shikishima* one of her forward 12-inch guns burst and another was for a time disabled. The *Asahi* had bursts in both her after turret guns due to over-heating. The Russians, except for the lagging *Poltava,* seemed quite unaffected by the Japanese fire as they steamed steadily on. The situation must have seemed calamitous to the Japanese commander; but then, at 6.40, with the sun hanging low over the western horizon, the whole picture was suddenly changed.

Vitgeft's flagship *Tzesarevitch,* was seen to swerve out of the line to port with a heavy list. Pouring smoke she circled right round until she charged through her own line ahead of the rear ship *Sevastopol.* Her engines were then stopped. The two 12-inch shells which had been the cause had lost the day for the Russians.

The first had burst near the foot of the mainmast. It had killed the Commander-in-Chief and sixteen others. The Chief of Staff and Flag Captain had been wounded and knocked senseless. The second shell had hit the conning tower, killing or stunning every man in it. The fleet was without a

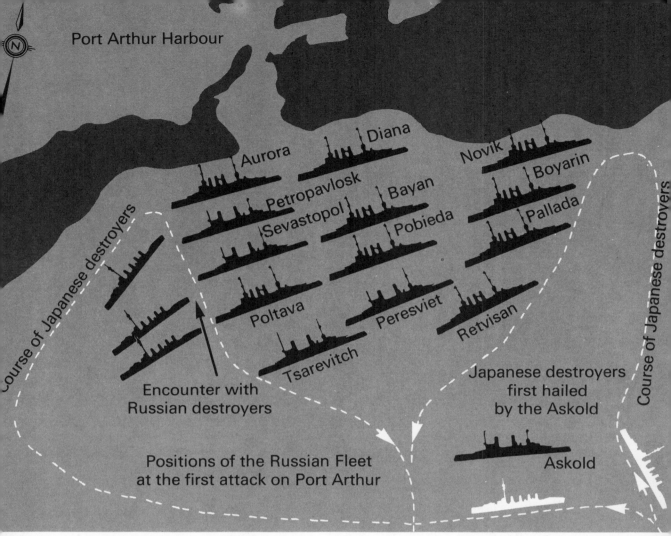

N

Course of Japanese destroyers

Aurora

Diana

Novik

Boyarin

Petropavlosk

Bayan

Sevastopol

Pobieda

Pallada

Poltava

Peresviet

Retvisan

Tsarevitch

Encounter with
Russian destroyers

Japanese destroyers
first hailed
by the Askold

Course of Japanese destroyers

Positions of the Russian Fleet
at the first attack on Port Arthur

Askold

leader. It began to dissolve into a milling throng. Togo turned to close in for the kill.

But before he could turn confusion into rout, there was to be one last heroic effort by the Russian fleet. The *Retvizan* next in the line to the *Tzesarevitch,* had followed her round, not at first realising she was out of control. She, in turn, was followed by the *Pobieda.* Together they charged the enemy to draw the fire away from the disabled flagship. As the *Retvizan* steered to ram the *Mikasa,* Togo was forced to give ground. Under the fire of every Japanese gun, the Russian ship plunged on. She had got to within a mile and a half of the Japanese flagship before a 12-inch shell struck home, forcing the *Retvizan*'s wounded captain to order his ship back to join the squadron.

His audacity had saved the Russian squadron from annihilation. It gave the *Tzesarevitch* and *Poltava* time to make repairs and get under way to follow the rest of the fleet making to the north-west to regain their base. Togo cannonading his defeated enemy, needed time in daylight to destroy him; but darkness was now descending. He dared not risk his precious battleships in a night action. Instead he unleashed his destroyers and torpedo-boats. These made repeated attacks throughout the night but to no avail.

By daybreak, five of the Russian battle-ships, a cruiser and three destroyers had reached Port Arthur. They were never to get to sea again, but would be eventually destroyed by the howitzer guns of the besieging Japanese armies. The flagship *Tzesarevitch,* the cruiser *Novik* and three

Right:
Admiral Togo's flagship, the *Mikasa*. Although faced by superior forces, the Russians were the first to draw blood, as two 12-inch shells smashed into the *Mikasa* causing damage and heavy casualties.

destroyers reached the neutral German port of Kiao-chao where they were interned. The cruiser *Askold* and another destroyer suffered the same fate at Shanghai, the cruiser *Diana* at Saigon.

It was the end of the Port Arthur squadron, though it was not until that fortress was captured in January 1905 that Togo realised it. But then he was able to have his fleet taken into dock for thorough repairs and refitting. Thus when the Russian Baltic Fleet, after a slow and difficult voyage half way round the world, arrived in the Straits of Tsu-shima on 27 May 1905, it was met by a Japanese fleet battle-worthy in every respect.

The Russian fleet on the other hand was in a dreadful state. The crews were untrained, coal cluttered the decks of the battleships, a number of old warships and transports slowed them down. The Battle of Tsu-shima which followed is much better known than that of the Yellow Sea. But it was, in fact, a one-sided battle resulting in the slaughter and destruction of almost all the Russian fleet at very little cost to the Japanese.

The Battle of the Yellow Sea was a much more vital encounter; the Japanese victory against a superior force ensured them control of the eastern seas and victory in the war. As a result of the Peace Treaty of Portsmouth, New Hampshire, which followed Tsu-shima, Japan's control of Korea was accepted. The Russian leasehold of Port Arthur and the peninsula on which it stood, and the railway and economic rights in Manchuria which the Russians had obtained from China, were transferred to Japan. The Japanese Empire had entered the front rank of Great Powers.

Jutland

31 May 1916

On the bridge of the battle-cruiser *Lion,* flagship of Vice-Admiral Sir David Beatty's Battle-Cruiser Fleet, there was an all too familiar feeling of disappointment at the apparent lack of achievement of yet another 'sweep' of the North Sea. The fleet, composed of six battle-cruisers, four new fast battleships, three light cruiser squadrons and three flotillas of destroyers, had sailed from its base at Rosyth in the Firth of Forth. At the same time the main body, the Grand Fleet, composed of twenty-four dreadnought battleships, three battle cruisers, three cruiser squadrons and three large flotillas of destroyers, had left its base, Scapa Flow, in the Orkney Islands.

It was 2.28 in the afternoon of 31 March 1916, a clear calm summer day, and Beatty's fleet had just turned from an easterly course towards the Skagerrak–the sea area between Denmark and Norway–to a northerly course. This was calculated to take them to meet the Grand Fleet. Led by the Commander-in-Chief, Admiral Sir John Jellicoe, flying his flag in the battleship *Iron Duke,* this was some 65 miles to the north, coming south to meet Beatty. Suddenly, on the *Lion*'s bridge there was an excited stir as a brief signal was reported. From the light-cruiser *Galatea,* scouting to the eastward–'Enemy in sight'.

Was this the great moment that all in the British fleet had been impatiently awaiting during the twenty months since the outbreak of the First World War? The German High Seas Fleet, considerably weaker than the Grand Fleet in dreadnoughts, which were the backbone of any fleet at that time, could not challenge its opponent at his full strength.

Up to now the Germans had contented themselves with 'tip and run' raids by their fast battle-cruisers to bombard English towns on the east coast. This had led to only one serious skirmish when Beatty's battle-cruisers had met them on 24 January 1915. The weaker German force had fled; in the running fight that followed, known as the Battle of the Dogger Bank, the German armoured cruiser *Blücher* had been sunk. The remainder had escaped, but both the *Lion* and the German battle-cruiser *Seydlitz* had suffered serious damage from the fire of their enemy's big guns.

Since then, the German Commander-in-Chief, Admiral Reinhard Scheer, had been pondering how he could lure the British to sea in such a way that the whole of his own fleet would be able to engage a portion of the enemy's. The plan he had decided upon was for his battle-cruiser force, commanded by Rear-Admiral Hipper, to steam north from the Heligoland Bight and let itself be seen off the Norwegian coast. Beatty's force would then come racing out from Rosyth to be trapped by Scheer with the main body of the High Seas Fleet, which would be secretly waiting some 40 miles to the southward. This was the plan which had been set on foot, with orders for Hipper to get under way at 1 a.m. on 31 May 1916.

Unfortunately for Scheer's plan, the British were able to read and decode many of the radio signals made to and by the High Seas Fleet. They knew well in advance that some big operation was to begin on the 31st. The Grand Fleet had been ordered to sea in good time to meet the Germans as they emerged through the barrier of minefields behind which they normally lurked. Nevertheless when, that afternoon, the *Galatea* came into view from Hipper's five battle-cruisers, it seemed to Scheer as though his plan was going to work.

Right, from Top to Bottom:
Vice-Admiral Beatty
Admiral Jellicoe
Admiral Scheer

Hipper, his flag flying in the battle-cruiser *Lützow,* steered in support of his scouts. When Beatty's big ships came into sight, the German admiral turned south to lure them towards Scheer's main body of battleships. Beatty turned, and as the two lines of big ships raced along on parallel courses at a range of 8¼ miles, the guns on either side thundered out. With six ships to the enemy's five, the British admiral had not felt it necessary to wait for his squadron of four fast battleships to catch up from their position astern of him on the new course.

This was to prove a bad mistake. For the German gunnery proved itself better than that of the British battle-cruisers, and Beatty's ships were soon suffering damage. And then a weakness in the design of their armour protection revealed itself in a shocking way as the *Indefatigable,* in the rear, suddenly staggered under the impact of two salvos from the *Von der Tann* and blew up, capsized and sank, taking all but two of her company of 1,017 with her.

The *Princess Royal* and the *Tiger* had also been hard hit, while the flagship *Lion* was ablaze and only saved from blowing up by flooding her forward magazine. Relief was coming, however.

The British squadron of fast battleships had been pelting forward at their utmost speed. Now, at last, they burst through the cloud of battle smoke hanging in the windless air to sight the enemy. Their 15-inch guns began to hurl accurate salvos of shells, each weighing one ton. It was the turn of Hipper's ships to suffer; though not as much as they might have done if the British shells had been better designed. As it was, some burst outside the German armour plates instead of penetrating it.

87

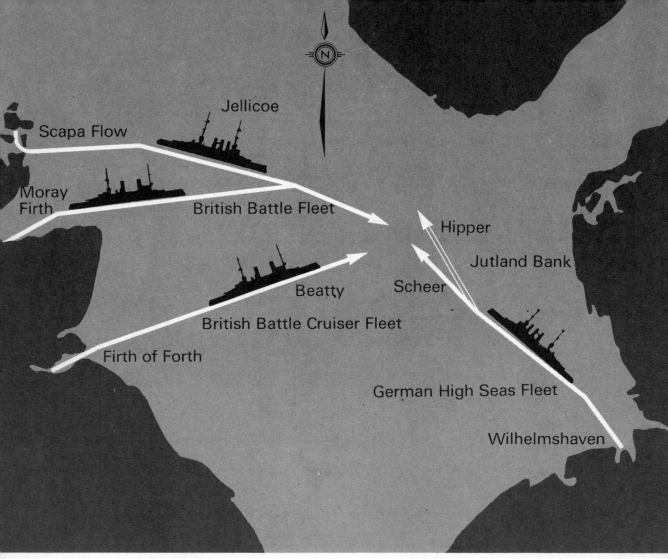

Jellicoe

Scapa Flow

Moray
Firth

British Battle Fleet

Hipper

Jutland Bank

Scheer

Beatty

British Battle Cruiser Fleet

Firth of Forth

German High Seas Fleet

Wilhelmshaven

And so, before the British gunfire could dominate the scene and force Hipper to turn away, Beatty's ships were to suffer another catastrophe. The *Queen Mary,* struck by five 12-inch shells in quick succession, went to her doom in the same way as the *Indefatigable.* In spite of this success on the part of the German battle-cruisers, they were by now in grave trouble from the growing damage caused by the British battleships. It was at this moment that a signal suddenly transformed the scene. The *Southampton,* scouting a few miles ahead of Beatty reported, 'Have sighted enemy battle fleet bearing S.E. Enemy's course north.'

Beatty was running headlong into the grasp of Scheer's fleet of sixteen dread-

noughts and six older battleships. There was not a moment to lose if he was to escape. The *Lion* swung round to the north followed by the remainder, already under long range fire from Scheer's van. Scheer's plan, it seemed, had worked. But in fact the situation had now been reversed.

As he and Hipper set out to chase Beatty northwards, they were, all unawares, running into Jellicoe's own trap. Hurrying through an increasing haze made thicker by drifting clouds of funnel and gun smoke, Scheer suddenly found the head of his line steering into the angle made by an L-shaped array of the greatly superior battle-ship force of the British Grand Fleet. From the dimly-seen shapes, ripples of yellow flashes told him that already salvos of 13·5 inch shells were hurtling towards his leading ships. Leaping pillars of water showed them falling dangerously close; hits would soon follow: there was only one thing he could do to escape: at a signal from his flagship, the *Friedrich der Grosse*, the whole long line of his battleships reversed course together and faded back into the haze.

It was a brilliantly executed manoeuvre which left Jellicoe groping blindly for the enemy who, a few moments earlier, had seemed doomed.

While this dramatic confrontation was taking place, the opposing light forces, scouting ahead of their respective fleets, had clashed in a fury of gun and torpedo fire. The British had been the losers in this exchange, losing a destroyer, the armoured cruiser *Defence* and the battle-cruiser *Invincible*. This last-named was one of three leading Jellicoe's line, which came up against the German battle-cruisers to suffer from the same design defect as her sisters in Beatty's force. The Germans lost only the cruiser *Wiesbaden*, but Hipper's battle-cruisers had suffered heavily, particularly his flagship, the *Lützow* which was in an almost sinking condition and was soon to crawl away out of action. She would later be abandoned and scuttled.

Scheer had for the moment successfully extricated himself from Jellicoe's deadly trap; but the British fleet was between him and his base. Miscalculating the situation, he now again reversed his line and headed north-eastwards in the expectation that this would enable him to cut across the stern of the Grand Fleet. Instead, out of the murk ahead of him there appeared the same interminable line of shadowy monsters and the ripple of gun flashes.

His situation was desperate. The devastating fire would soon destroy his battle-cruisers and the dreadnoughts at the head of his line unless he took desperate measures to get out of it. To his battle-cruisers, now led by the *Derfflinger,* he signalled for them to charge the enemy in what was to be known as their 'death-ride'. His destroyers he ordered to deliver a massed torpedo attack on the Grand Fleet battle squadrons. Under cover of these diversions he once again reversed course.

With great gallantry the battle-cruisers obeyed the order to sacrifice themselves. They were cruelly hammered by the British gunfire; but their own stout construction and the fatal flaw in the British shells saved them from destruction. It was the attack by the destroyers, however, which was to save Scheer. Thirteen of these little craft fired 28 torpedoes. To avoid them Jellicoe turned his battle fleet 45 degrees away from the enemy. The two fleets were thus opening out from one another at a speed of some 20 knots. Soon they were out of sight and touch with one another. By the time the threat from torpedoes was over, the sun was setting in the west and only an hour or two of daylight remained.

Had the Grand Fleet been turned back at once to a westerly course, the battle might have been renewed in time to bring about a decisive end. But Jellicoe, who had so skilfully trapped Scheer, was not prepared to take risks with the Grand Fleet to finish him off. Uncertain of the enemy's position and course, unwilling to expose his ships to the risk of torpedo fire from the enemy's battleships, from a submarine 'ambush' or a mine trap, he hesitated. And as Jellicoe was determined to avoid a night action which always favoured the smaller

and more controllable force, he let the chance of victory slip through his fingers.

Nevertheless, at nightfall on 31 May the Grand Fleet was still between the High Seas Fleet and its base. Jellicoe's plan was to keep it so and renew the battle at daylight. Scheer, with his battle-cruisers and the three leading ships of his dreadnought line heavily damaged, and outnumbered, was desperate to avoid a further trial of strength. He would rather risk a violent break through the enemy fleet during the night. As darkness fell, therefore, he radioed a course for the Horn's Reef Light Vessel, the entrance to one of the two swept channels through the minefields. He added the stern order, 'This course is to be maintained.'

Jellicoe, on the other hand, felt he had to cover both that route and another which Scheer might take through the minefields,

much further south. He therefore set a course and speed which would keep the battle fleet athwart the more southerly route. Astern of the battleships he massed his huge destroyer force, much of which had as yet done no fighting. Night action, with torpedoes being fired at close range was their accepted role. Jellicoe evidently felt sure that this would be sufficient to stop Scheer crossing astern of him to reach Horn's Reef.

He was to be grievously disappointed. Throughout the night, far behind the battle fleet, flotilla after flotilla encountered the German battleship line. They were met by an immensely well practised night-fighting technique and driven off with losses. Of the torpedoes they fired, only two found a target, sinking the cruiser *Rostock* and the old battleship *Pommern*. Another cruiser, the *Elbing* was rammed and sunk by the

German battleship *Posen* as she was turning to avoid torpedoes.

Nevertheless, all this activity – searchlight beams, gunflashes – was visible from at least the rear units of Jellicoe's battleships. No-one thought to tell the Admiral. On the other hand, the Admiralty had intercepted Scheer's message giving his fleet their course for the night. They had passed the news on to the Commander-in-Chief. And though they foolishly failed to pass an even more informative message intercepted – a request by Scheer for Zeppelin airships to meet him at Horn's Reef – this should have made the situation clear. But Jellicoe steamed steadily on while the enemy cut across in rear of him.

By the morning Scheer had slipped out of the trap and was approaching the protection of his minefields. The Battle of Jutland was over. Both sides were to claim

victory; the Germans because they had encountered and escaped from a greatly superior fleet, having sunk more ships than they themselves had lost; the British because they had driven the Germans back into harbour, never again to risk action with the Grand Fleet.

It is probably true to say that neither side could claim a victory. British losses were three battle cruisers, three armoured cruisers and eight destroyers. The Germans lost only the battle-cruiser *Lützow*, the battleship *Pommern*, four light cruisers and five destroyers. Nevertheless the outcome of the battle was to convince Admiral Scheer that there could be no idea of ever again risking a fleet action. The German Navy from this time onwards was to rely upon its submarines waging war on its enemies' merchant ships to counteract British seapower.

The Battle of
the Atlantic

1939-1943

Previous Page:
A typical Atlantic convoy and escort during the
Second World War.

Below:
This is a IX B class submarine. Its maximum speed
was 18·2 knots and had a surface range of 12,000
miles at 10 knots, falling to 3,800 miles at maximum
speed.

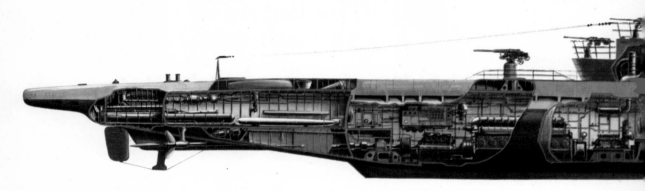

Britain's greatest strength in face of her
enemies has always been that she is an
island. Any foe, in order to subdue her,
would have to send an army across the
stretch of stormy sea known as the English
Channel. So long as the Royal Navy was
supreme at sea, this was not possible.

But Britain grew from a small farming
nation into a nation of engineers and
merchants. To feed her people and to carry
on the trade by which she paid for their
food, she had to build and operate a large
number of merchant ships. The largest
merchant fleet in the world sailed under
the British flag. Britain's enemies saw that
by sinking these ships they could starve
and ruin her just as well as by invasion of
the British Isles.

In the two great World Wars of the
twentieth century, these enemies were the
Germans. In the first of these (1914-1918),
unable to match the power of Britain on
the surface of the seas, they made use of
the newly-perfected type of warship, the
submarine. Sent out to lurk near the busy
parts of the shipping routes, they were able
to stop ship after ship and, after ordering
their crews into the boats, send them to
the bottom. By submerging they were able
to escape the patrolling warships trying in
vain to hunt them.

Efforts to find a means of detecting and
attacking them under water were unsuccessful. When the British and their
allies gave each merchant ship a gun with
which to defend itself, the U-boats, as the
German submarines were known, attacked
with torpedoes from under the surface and
without warning.

Now the merchant ships were sunk at an
ever-increasing rate. In spite of a huge
force of fast patrol craft scouring the seas,
few U-boats were sunk in reply. By 1917,
Great Britain was within sight of defeat by
starvation. Then came salvation. It came
to be realised that the answer to the U-boat
challenge was to sail ships in large groups
or convoys; each convoy was given escort
by warships, aeroplanes and airships. This
greatly reduced the number of targets for
the U-boats to find. It also forced the submarines to come in amongst their most
dangerous foes, the escort, if they wished
to achieve anything.

The result was a dramatic drop in the
number of merchant ships being sunk, and
a sharp rise in the number of U-boats
meeting that fate themselves. Never again
in that war did Germany come near to
defeating the Allies at sea. Before it ended,
scientists had at last invented a means of
detecting submerged U-boats by sending

out a sound beam and listening for its echo to return after bouncing off a U-boat's hull. This was called the 'Asdic' but today is more usually referred to as 'Sonar'. In combination with the depth-charge—a large can filled with explosive which could be set to burst at any chosen depth—a means of sinking U-boats without ever seeing them had been found.

So when war between Great Britain and the Germany led by Adolf Hitler broke out in September 1939, it was believed that a convoy system with escorts fitted with asdic would be a sound defence.

Unfortunately, during the years of peace, the people of Britain had closed their eyes to the threat of war by Germany. Their government refused to vote the money needed to build the escorts. Unfortunately also for Britain and her allies, the Germans discovered that the asdic could not detect a U-boat on the surface; and as they also found that by night a U-boat could not be seen from the bridge of a ship, they were able to slip in the darkness between the very few escorts that could be allotted to each convoy and get amongst the merchantmen to loose their torpedoes.

Their next idea was to attack in groups of several U-boats working together. These came to be known as wolf-packs. The first

U-boat to locate a convoy would signal its position. Others would then gather ahead of it and, after dark, move in. The escorts found themselves overwhelmed. Ship after ship in the convoy sent distress rockets soaring up into the night sky to signal that they had been torpedoed. But all the escorts could do was to rescue as many crew survivors as possible from their lifeboats or from the sea. The U-boats escaped unharmed. In the autumn of 1940, convoys thus assailed often lost almost half their numbers.

Before we continue with the story, we should look at the type of ships involved on either side. The U-boats were quite small craft of 800 and 1,200 tons. In the narrow, cigar-shaped hull, a maze of pipes and electric mains; a huge battery of massive electric storage cells providing power to drive the boat under water; two powerful diesel engines to drive it on the surface and to charge the electric batteries through dynamos; a cluster of four or five torpedo tubes in the bow and one or two in the stern, with spare torpedoes; and, amidships a control room from where the boat was steered and dived, and where the steel columns of the two periscopes with the eyepieces at the bottom end were hoisted up and down by electric power.

95

Right:
This map shows the extent of the Black Gap—that part of the Atlantic Ocean without any air-cover. It was in the Black Gap that convoys were most vulnerable to attack from U-boat wolf-packs.

In the cramped space left by all this, some forty-eight officers and men worked, ate and slept for several weeks at a time. When on the surface, there was room for the captain, an officer of the watch and four look-outs on the top deck of the conning tower. There they had scant shelter from the wind and the spray thrown up as the little ships plunged and rolled in the Atlantic waves.

When they dived, however, the U-boats escaped the wicked Atlantic weather and enjoyed the quiet calm of the depths. It was otherwise with their enemies, the escorts. Riding the huge, spray-lashed, foaming Atlantic rollers, life was a misery whether on the wind-swept bridges or in the steel-walled mess-decks, where water sloshed to and fro across the deck.

Three types of ship were mainly involved. 'Destroyers' built for speed; 'sloops' or 'frigates', more roomy and less austere, but not so fast; and 'corvettes', little bluff vessels which could be built easily and quickly, but so slow that they could not catch a submarine on the surface. The long, lean hulls of the destroyers, half out of the water as they climbed over the great waves, swooped sickeningly to hit the following crests with crashes that shook them from end to end. But in fair weather they could race at the speed of an express train to catch a reported U-boat. The sloops and corvettes wallowed and rolled till all but the strongest stomachs prayed for relief; but they could get about and around during storms in a way often impossible to the destroyers.

Such were the warships on either side which fought the Battle of the Atlantic. Both sides were supported as far as possible by their air forces. Scouting for the U-boats as well as bombing ships in the convoys,

were large four-engined Focke-Wulf Condor planes. Aircraft of Coastal Command of the Royal Air Force helped the convoy escorts.

To protect the convoys, two main things were needed to combat the U-boat tactics.

The first was to make it dangerous for the submarines to come to the surface during daylight, either to re-charge their electric storage batteries on which they ran submerged, or to catch the convoys; they were too slow under water to do this without surfacing. So the answer took the form of patrolling aircraft. These, too, like the escorts were woefully few in number. Only a handful of big Sunderland flying boats were available to fly any distance out into the Atlantic. Most of the planes flown by the Royal Air Force's Coastal Command could only support the convoy escorts for about 150 miles from our coasts.

This air effort was enough to force the U-boats to operate farther afield. But it also meant that the convoys needed escort for longer on their voyage. This in turn called for more escorts which at first simply did not exist. Not until air and surface escort could be provided throughout the voyage would the means of beating the wolf-packs be really found.

The other vital need was to find a way of detecting the U-boats on the surface during the night. Such 'a magic eye' which could detect aircraft by the use of radio pulses in much the same way as the asdic used sound waves, had been devised before the war. But the British had not been able to adapt this system to detecting ships. Scientists were at work on this problem, but not until early 1941 was the first primitive and not very useful type of · what is today called 'radar' provided. It

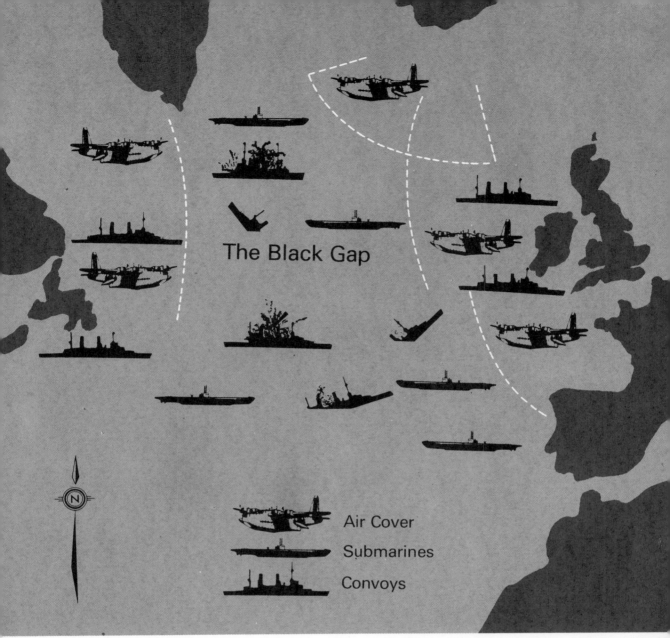

The Black Gap

Air Cover

Submarines

Convoys

would be some time before a ship-borne or airborne radar could detect a surfaced submarine at two or three miles range.

Another threat to allied merchant shipping in the Atlantic was presented by German surface warships which succeeded in evading British patrols in the north to break out past Iceland. For a while they would cause painful losses; but their careers were short. They were either brought to book, like the 'pocket battleship' *Admiral Graf Spee* in the Battle of the River Plate (December 1939) or the huge

Bismarck (May 1941); or, like the battleships *Scharnhorst* and *Gneisenau* they were kept unfit for action by R.A.F. raids on the port of Brest where they had been forced to go for fuel and repairs. Thus they were never as great a menace as the sinister, elusive U-boats.

The Germans had started the war with only twenty-seven ocean-going types of these and thirty smaller North Sea boats. They strained every nerve to build up their numbers. So, too, did the British, to produce more escorts and to build merchant ships to replace those sunk. A race developed in which the advantage went first to one side, then the other. By March 1941 it was beginning to favour the British. Many of the new escorts, the corvettes, all named after flowers, had come to sea. Their crews had gained experience and training. R.A.F. Coastal Command had more planes and of longer range to harry the wolf-packs to some extent. And in that month the U-boat command suffered a severe setback. Their three most successful and famous captains were either drowned or captured when their craft were destroyed by depth-charges as they attacked convoys.

Greatly alarmed, the Germans sent their submarines yet further out into the Atlantic to seek their prey. This forced the British to provide escort aircraft as well as surface ships, ever farther also. Bases and airfields had to be set up in Iceland and eventually in Newfoundland and Nova Scotia to provide, with the help of the growing Canadian Navy, escort clear across the ocean. On the route southwards to the Orient via the Cape of Good Hope, convoys needed escort and a base was set up at Freetown, Sierra Leone.

A factor favouring the British at this time was American aid in escorting convoys between the United States and Iceland. Though the former were still officially neutral they had taken over the defence of Iceland in July 1941.

During the latter half of 1941, new radar sets were being fitted in British escorts and aircraft to even the odds against the U-boats by night. Improved asdic sets and more effective depth charges made the destruction of submerged submarines less difficult. Though the number of U-boats in service had increased to two hundred,

Hitler ordered the majority to be sent to the Mediterranean, against the advice of his U-boat Admiral, Doenitz. So the battle was moving steadily in favour of the escorts.

In December there was a notable victory by the escort of a convoy from Gibraltar, commanded by Captain F. J. Walker. Taking part in this six-day battle was the first escort aircraft-carrier, HMS *Audacity,* converted from a captured merchant ship. With the aid of her aircraft and as a result of the careful training Walker gave to his team of escorts, four German U-boats and two large enemy aircraft scouting for them were destroyed. Only two ships of the convoy were lost. And though a destroyer escort and the *Audacity* herself were also sunk during the battle, the outcome was admitted by Admiral Doenitz, to be an alarming defeat of his forces. Captain 'Johnnie' Walker was to go on to become the greatest scourge of the U-boats during the next three years.

But at this moment the pendulum of fortune swung swiftly back in Doenitz's favour. Following Japan's attack, the United States of America entered the war on Britain's side. In the long run, of course, this was to ensure Allied victory as the immense power and wealth of America swung into action. But at first its effect on the Battle of the Atlantic was only to expose to the U-boat attacks the throng of shipping using the previously neutral waters of the American east coast.

In spite of the lessons learned by the British in two World Wars, the Americans were not convinced that only a convoy system could defend it. And in the next six months, undeterred by aircraft and destroyers patrolling the route, U-boats sank some five hundred ships as they steamed along the regular routes in sight of American coastal towns. Most of them were carrying oil, munitions and raw materials vital for Britain to carry on the war and food to feed her people.

When at last the lesson was learned and a convoy system for the whole Atlantic organised, the U-boats turned away to seek the weakest section of this system. Out in the middle of the storm-swept Atlantic was an area known to the escorts as the 'Black Gap' where air escort could only be given by big, four-engined planes, with fuel capacity specially increased for very long range patrolling. So few of these had been allocated that the convoys had usually to cross the 'Black Gap' without their aid. The U-boats were thus left free, as earlier in the war, to gather into wolf-packs. Twenty or more of them might fall upon a convoy at one time, swamping the half a dozen escorts thinly spread round the five or six square miles that the convoy covered.

Through the autumn and winter of 1942 the battle raged in full fury. The long, black nights were time and again made hideous by the flames of burning tankers, the numbing thud of exploding torpedoes and too often the despairing cries of sailors left to drown. The U-boats paid a painful price for their successes, as some of them were detected by radar, forced to dive and then hunted to their death by asdic and depth-charges. But on the whole the advantage lay with them. It might have continued to do so had it not been that a number of decisive steps being taken by the Allies were about to take effect.

Firstly, the number of escorts available had greatly increased, so that in addition to the old experienced groups which formed the close guard round every convoy, new Support Groups could be formed. These were sent to back up the escorts of any convoy threatened with a wolf-pack attack. Secondly, every escort was by now fitted with the most up-to-date radar which made it almost impossible for a U-boat to approach by night on the surface undetected. A number of escorts also had a radio direction finding set with which the direction of any U-boat reporting to base could be discovered. Thus any signal – and to operate the wolf-packs many signals were essential – might bring down on the U-boat the racing knife-edge of a vengeful destroyer's stem.

Finally, the 'Black Gap' was about to be closed. Not only had more very long range aircraft been provided for Coastal Command of the RAF, but naval planes were able to accompany the convoys all the time.

They took off and landed on the decks of little escort carriers, successors to the *Audacity* mentioned earlier. Now the U-boats found themselves being pounced on and harrassed whenever they came to the surface. Many were sunk or damaged as planes swooped down to drop depth charges round them. Others were time and again frustrated as they tried to get into position to attack a convoy.

All these new influences were brought into play in the Spring of 1943. Although in April no less than ninety-eight U-boats left their bases to gather on the convoy routes, again and again they found themselves frustrated; many were lost. Not yet, however, did they acknowledge defeat. At the beginning of May as many as sixty U-boats took part in an eight-day battle round a slow outward-bound convoy. Though the escorts detected, intercepted and drove off

U-boat after U-boat, sinking one and damaging more, others got through to send eleven merchant ships to the bottom. But then the wild weather which had favoured the U-boats gave way to a fog-shrouded calm. The escorts' radar now reversed the advantage. One after the other, U-boats were surprised on the surface. One was rammed and cut in half by a destroyer; others were depth-charged to destruction; many were so damaged that they had to limp away for home.

When the remainder finally gave up, five U-boats had been sunk by the escorts, one by a Royal Canadian Air Force plane; two others hurrying through the fog had collided and sunk. Such losses were too great to be borne; the U-boat crews surviving were very demoralised. Though they returned to the attack during May they achieved almost nothing, and by the end of the month twenty-five had been caught and destroyed round the convoys. A further six were surprised at night by radar-fitted planes as they travelled on the surface through the Bay of Biscay to and from their base at Lorient. In all, forty-one were lost during May.

Admiral Doenitz, who had lost a son in one of them, accepted defeat and recalled all the survivors from the North Atlantic convoy routes. Though the U-boats would go on fighting to the end of the war with a courage their enemies could only admire, never again were they to be the mortal threat they had become at the beginning of 1943.

But let it not be forgotten that it was Britain's great war leader, Winston Churchill, who wrote: 'The only thing that ever really frightened me during the war was the U-boat peril.'

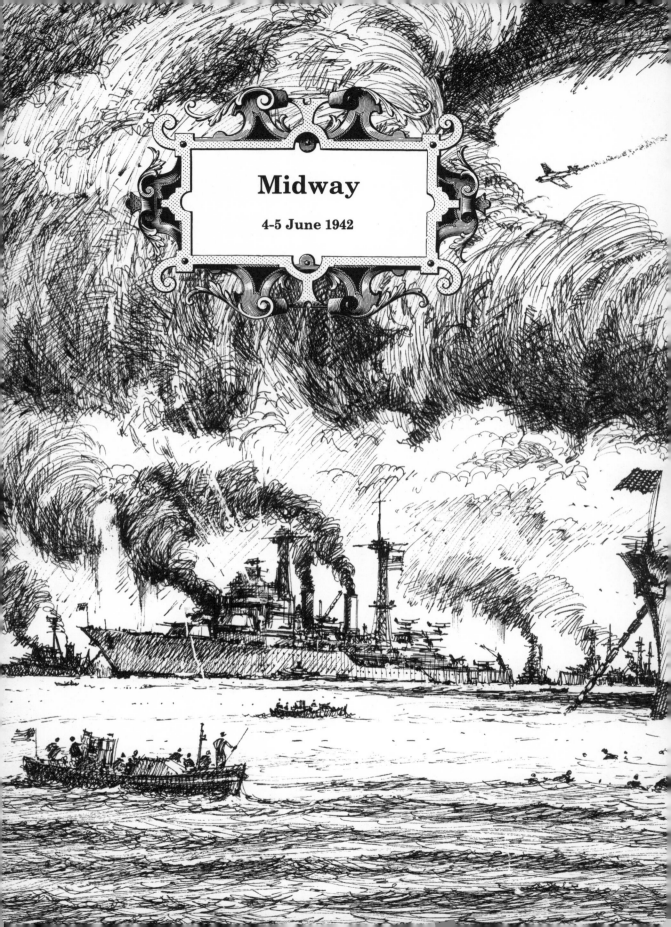

Midway

4-5 June 1942

On 7 December 1941, a sleepy, sunny, tropical Sunday morning at the United States Naval Base, Pearl Harbor, in the Hawaiian Islands had been suddenly transformed into a horror of explosion and fire. From a swarm of aircraft which had taken off from a Japanese force of six carriers, bombs and torpedoes had eliminated the seven battleships forming the hard core of the U.S. Pacific Fleet. Thus Japan had declared war upon the U.S.A. At about the same time, Japanese troops tumbling ashore from transports on to the Malay Peninsula had similarly challenged the British Empire.

For the next five months the war had gone entirely in favour of the Japanese. Malaya, Singapore, the Philippine Islands, the Dutch East Indies, the Bismarck Island Group: all had fallen to their attacks. The limits of the Japanese Empire had been pushed outwards to contain the sources of oil, tin, rubber and rice, so vital to the war effort. In accordance with their war plan the Japanese should then have halted, strengthened their defences and defied the enemy to dislodge them. But over-confidence, bred by easy victories drove them to further expansion.

In the south they launched an expedition aimed at capturing Port Moresby on the south coast of Papua. From here, they could threaten Australia. This led to the Battle of the Coral Sea, 4/7 May, 1942. It resulted in the loss of the American carrier *Lexington,* and damage to the carrier *Yorktown,* against the loss of the light carrier *Shoho* and heavy damage to the carrier *Shokaku* of their opponents. The Japanese also lost a great many of their experienced airmen, who could not quickly be replaced, from their carriers *Shokaku* and *Zuikaku*. More important than these losses on either side, the Japanese expansion in the south was halted.

Nevertheless the Japanese determined to carry on with their plan to push their frontiers outwards in the north by capturing the Aleutian Islands and Midway, the most northerly of the long chain of Hawaiian Islands. It was an ambitious plan, using almost the whole of the Japanese Fleet. But the *Shokaku* and her sister ship would be absent, still re-equipping and repairing after the Coral Sea Battle. A squadron, including two auxiliary aircraft carriers, backed by four battleships was to sail against the Aleutians.

For the assault on Midway there would be the main Japanese aircraft-carrier striking force, *Akagi,* flagship of Vice-Admiral Nagumo, *Kaga, Soryu* and *Hiryu* with an escort of battleships, cruisers and destroyers, to batter Midway from the air at dawn on 4 June 1942. They also had the task of discovering and attacking the American carrier squadron which was expected to come out from Pearl Harbor. The difficulty of one force taking care of these two separate tasks, was to be the key to the events about to unfold.

In addition to this striking force, there was the Transport Unit of six troopships, supported by a squadron of two battleships, cruisers and destroyers, and another squadron of heavy cruisers to bombard Midway; finally there was the main body of the fleet, centred on the *Yamato,* largest battleship in the world, and flagship of the Commander-in-Chief, Admiral Yamamoto, and six other battleships.

The various Japanese units followed widely separated routes to the area north of Midway, but they added up to an

Right, from Top to Bottom:
Admiral Yamamoto
Vice-Admiral Nagumo
Admiral Nimitz
Rear-Admiral Fletcher

impressive strength. Yamamoto believed that the Americans had only two carriers available in the north to oppose him. He also thought they would be taken by surprise and so would not be able to appear on the scene until the assault on Midway was over. He could be forgiven for thinking that they must be overwhelmed by his own superior force. In addition, he ordered a barrier of submarines to be established between Pearl Harbor and Midway on 3 June. He believed the Americans would have to pass through this barrier when they came out of Pearl Harbor. The Japanese admiral was to find himself mistaken on each count.

Unknown to him, the Americans had for some time been able to intercept and de-code Japanese naval signals. So they knew in advance the main details of the Midway plan. Admiral Nimitz, the Commander-in-Chief, Pacific, had recalled to Pearl Harbor all his three carriers remaining after the Coral Sea Battle. The *Enterprise,* flagship of Rear-Admiral Spruance and the *Hornet,* which had not taken part, were fully battle-ready, and sailed on 28 May for an area north-east of Midway. The *Yorktown,* flag-ship of Rear-Admiral Fletcher, hastily repaired, got away on the 30th. Two days later the three carriers joined up under Fletcher's command, ready to meet the threat they knew was approaching. Un-known to Yamamoto, they were thus through the Japanese submarine trap before it had been formed.

The tiny island of Midway was laid out as an air base. On its airfield were based twenty-one U.S. Army bombers and tor-pedo planes, twenty-seven fighters, thirty dive-bombers of the Marine Corps and six U.S. Navy torpedo planes. From the lagoon

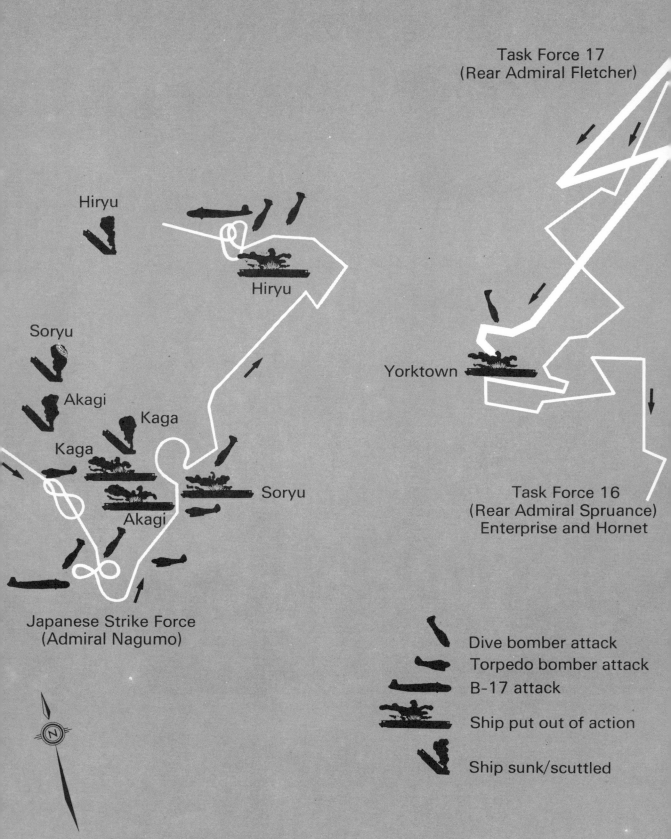

Task Force 17
(Rear Admiral Fletcher)

Hiryu

Hiryu

Yorktown

Soryu

Akagi

Kaga

Kaga

Soryu

Akagi

Task Force 16
(Rear Admiral Spruance)
Enterprise and Hornet

Japanese Strike Force
(Admiral Nagumo)

N

Dive bomber attack

Torpedo bomber attack

B-17 attack

Ship put out of action

Ship sunk/scuttled

Left:
This map shows the course of the Battle of Midway.
This decisive naval battle was fought entirely by
aircraft from carriers—no ship directly engaged
another.

inside the coral reefs a squadron of Catalina flying boats operated. This might seem a powerful air force; but the airmen were only partly trained and were inexperienced; the fighter planes were out of date and would be outclassed by Japanese naval planes.

Such was the situation when, early on 3 June, a Catalina on regular scouting duty from Midway discovered the approaching Japanese Transport Unit some 650 miles to the west of the island. Over the radio flashed the news; U.S. Army bombers took off to attack; they failed to achieve anything though they believed they had hit ships which they reported as battleships and cruisers. Catalinas armed with torpedoes did little better, though they did slightly damage a tanker.

Meanwhile, under the cover of a blanket of low cloud and thick weather, Nagumo's carriers were approaching undiscovered. At dawn on the 4th, they steamed into clear weather and his air striking force roared off the carrier decks and headed for Midway—seventy-two bombers escorted by thirty-six of the famous Zero fighters. They were seen and reported by a scouting Catalina and soon afterwards the carriers themselves were also sighted. Thus the island's defending fighters were in the air in good time to meet the attackers, only to be almost all shot down by the Zeros. The bombers went on to make havoc of the Midway base. In reply, the island's bombers and torpedo planes had been attacking the Japanese carriers, all to no avail and at heavy loss to themselves.

On board his flagship, Admiral Nagumo had been anxiously awaiting signals from two sources—from the leader of the bombers to say if a second attack wave was neces-

sary, and from the seven sea-planes which had flown off his cruisers to scout to the eastward. The bombers of the second wave waiting to take off had been armed with torpedoes in case an enemy fleet was discovered by the float-planes which, of course, would be useless against Midway. Nothing had come in from the seaplanes, when a signal calling for a second strike on Midway was received. Nagumo ordered the bombers to be taken down in the lifts from the flight decks to the hangars to have bombs fitted in place of their torpedoes.

Thirteen minutes later a seaplane from one of the cruisers sent the startling news of an enemy force 300 miles to the eastward.

Now the Japanese admiral was in a fix. He hastily stopped the change in armament of his bombers, and gave orders for the planes to be ranged up on deck again. But before he could launch them and send them against the American ships, the series of attacks by Midway bombers began. His Zero fighters were flown off to deal with the attackers; but for the next half hour his carriers were too busy weaving this way and that, avoiding bombs and torpedoes, for any bombers to be flown off against the enemy fleet. Then the aircraft returning from Midway had to be given clear decks on which to land. Nagumo was faced with two alternatives. Either the second wave of bombers could be flown off to the attack, but without fighter escort—because the Zeros needed now to re-fuel—or they must be sent down to the hangars.

Nagumo made the fateful decision to send them down. In that moment the Battle of Midway was lost and won.

For unknown to the Japanese, sixty-eight dive-bombers and twenty-nine

Previous Page:
Dive bombers led by Commander Clarence
McCluskey of the *Enterprise* and
Lieutenant-Commander Maxwell P. Leslie of the
Yorktown formed the attack on the main Japanese
carrier force. This picture shows Leslie's dive
bombers attacking the *Kaga,* and with four direct
hits, reducing her to a blazing wreck.

torpedo-planes from the *Enterprise* and *Hornet,* followed by seventeen dive-bombers and twelve torpedo-planes from the *Yorktown,* were on their way. They were due to arrive while the Japanese carriers were still frenziedly occupied in receiving their aircraft, sending them down to the hangars to be re-fuelled and re-armed.

The Americans had received the news of Nagumo's squadron while scouts from the *Yorktown* were still away. Realising that not a moment should be lost, Admiral Fletcher ordered Spruance to take the other two carriers away to the south-west and fly off their striking force. He would follow in the *Yorktown* as soon as she had gathered in her scouts and would fly off a second strike from her.

The planes from *Enterprise* and *Hornet* flew in several groups, and on various routes. The *Hornet's* dive-bombers and fighters flew to intercept the enemy carriers assuming they would continue to steam in the direction they were heading when reported. So, too, did the dive-bombers of the *Enterprise.* But Nagumo had, in fact, turned sharply north-east; so no enemy was in sight when expected. The *Hornet's* planes made a wrong choice and turned south to search. They thus flew out of the battle altogether, ending up in the sea when their fuel ran out, or on Midway, or back at their carrier. The *Enterprise's* dive-bombers led by Commander Clarence McCluskey turned north, a choice that was to bring him fame and glory.

For the longer route he had followed was to bring him in sight of the enemy carriers soon after the slower torpedo squadrons from *Enterprise* and *Hornet* had made their attack, and while the *Yorktown's* were still launching their torpedoes at the swerving, twisting Japanese ships. The first two of these squadrons had attacked without any fighter support because, by some mistake, the ten escorting Wildcats from the *Enterprise* were not called down from their position high above the battle to take part. Everyone of the torpedo planes had been shot down. So had all but two of the *Yorktown's* torpedo planes, in spite of valiant efforts by their own fighter escort. No torpedo hits were made.

At this stage, the battle was a disaster for the Americans. Wild cheers from the Japanese sailors greeted their own success; on their decks their own striking force was now ranged up and almost ready to go.

Suddenly there was heard the spine-chilling, whining scream of diving planes. From high up in the sky, where the Japanese had not seen them, the dive-bombers of McCluskey and others from the *Yorktown* led by Lieutenant-Commander Maxwell P. Leslie, were plummeting down at their targets.

Leslie's squadron was the first to attack. Four direct hits on the *Kaga* reduced her in a few minutes to a blazing wreck as petrol poured from broken pipes to feed the flames. McCluskey's men dived soon after, selecting the flagship *Akagi* and the *Soryu.* Both were fatally damaged, though it would not be until the evening that they would finally sink. Nagumo and his staff had to transfer to a cruiser. Only the *Hiryu* of his carrier squadron was still in operation and undamaged, because she had become somewhat separated from the remainder.

From her deck rose a gallant little striking force of eighteen dive-bombers and six fighter escorts. Following the home-ward-bound American planes they were led to the *Yorktown*. Radar (radio detecting device) detected them when still 50 miles away; defending Wildcat fighters swooped and shot down all but eight of the bombers. Three more fell to the *Yorktown*'s guns; but five pressed bravely on and scored three hits. They were not fatal, however, and soon, with her decks patched up, the carrier was again operating her planes.

But now the *Hiryu*'s torpedo planes, ten in number, arrived in their turn. Five were shot down before they could launch their missiles, but two of the others scored hits, tearing open the ship's hull. Through the gash the sea poured giving her a steep list. The order was given to abandon ship though, in fact, the *Yorktown* was far from doomed yet. At this same moment the *Hiryu* was at last located by American scout planes. The final moment of retribution for the treacherous attack on Pearl Harbor was at hand.

From the *Enterprise,* twenty-four dive-bombers, led by Lieutenant Gallaher; from the *Hornet,* sixteen more, took off and winged their way across the sea. It was Gallaher's men who arrived first, and diving steeply over the Japanese carrier scored four direct hits, reducing the *Hiryu* to a shattered wreck that was to burn uncontrollably for eleven hours, before being finally abandoned and sent to the bottom by Japanese torpedoes at 4.30 the following morning.

Four of the six carriers of Nagumo's squadron, which had made the Pearl Harbor attack and, during the next six months, had ranged unchallenged over the eastern seas, had been destroyed. The other two were the *Shokaku* and *Zuikaku*.

Though the attack on the Aleutians had been successful and the islands of Kiska and Attu occupied by the Japanese, Admiral Yamamoto was forced to recognise that his fleet had suffered a shattering defeat. All the mighty strength of his battleships with their huge guns was of no use against the American carriers which could hold off and despatch their bombers from hundreds of miles away. He recalled all his units and turned back to Japan.

Yamamoto had lost, partly through the technical skill of his opponents in breaking the Japanese secret codes; partly through over-confidence leading to a failure to concentrate his forces against the chance of attack by the enemy's aircraft. Had his seven battleships and numerous cruisers and destroyers, hovering uselessly far from the scene, been there to protect his carriers with their massed gunfire, the outcome might have been very different.

The Americans, apart from the tragic loss of their torpedo squadrons which had attacked so heroically against odds, had not escaped scot-free. The *Yorktown,* heavily damaged, had been taken in tow and was limping painfully towards Pearl Harbor when a Japanese submarine intercepted her, and sent her finally to the bottom with two torpedo hits. Nevertheless the balance of power in the Pacific War which had been so much in the Japanese favour, had been evened out. And soon, with the arrival of new carriers and battleships being built in the United States, the Americans would be able to go over from defence to attack.

The Battle of Midway was thus a great turning point in the Second World War.

The Battle for Leyte Gulf

23-25 October 1944

As a result of the Battle of Midway, the Japanese had been halted in their efforts to expand their conquests further. For the remainder of 1942 this situation was maintained with the Anglo-American Allies just strong enough to hold the Japanese in check.

By the spring of 1943, however, the Allies had sufficiently recovered and assembled forces to begin driving the Japanese out of their conquered lands. Slowly but steadily they had been pushed back and evicted from the Solomon Island chain by American naval and military forces; while American and Australian troops under the American General MacArthur had retaken Papua and advanced up the north coast of New Guinea. By November 1943 the American Pacific Fleet had been strengthened by the addition of the first of the splendid new carriers, each able to operate scores of dive-bombers, torpedo planes and fighters from its deck, and by new battleships, which had been first laid down before the outbreak of war. New thrusts were now possible to re-capture the Gilberts, the Marshalls and the Marianas.

These operations had been most successful; costly defeats had been inflicted on the Japanese, particularly off the Marianas, where in the huge carrier battle of the Philippine Sea, Japanese naval air power had been almost wiped out. This enabled the U.S. Navy to send an American army in a vast fleet of transports to land in the Gulf of Leyte to begin the reconquest of the Philippine Islands on 20 October 1944.

Providing naval support for this great armada was a force of six battleships—old and slow, but suitable with their 16-inch or 14-inch guns for shore bombardment or defence against surface attack – eight cruisers, including the Australian *Shropshire* and twenty-seven American and one Australian destroyer. Giving close air support to the landed troops was a force of eighteen escort carriers divided into three groups of six with a screen of destroyers. Each carrier, a converted merchant ship with an armament of only a single 5-inch gun, had some twelve Avenger torpedo-bombers and twelve to eighteen Hellcat or Wildcat fighters embarked. From their decks, as they operated out in the Philippine Sea to the eastward of Samar Island, the Avengers were directed to bombing missions against Japanese defending troops, and the fighters to give protection against enemy air attacks.

Together with the hundreds of transports and landing ships, these forces comprised the U.S. Seventh Fleet under Vice-Admiral T. C. Kinkaid. Additional support was also being supplied by the U.S. Third Fleet under Admiral W. F. Halsey. This consisted of Task Force 38, organised and divided into four Task Groups in each of which were four or five aircraft carriers. Group No. 1 had been detached to the fleet's advanced base in the Carolines to refuel, replenish and rest; so the aircraft left in the Task Force numbered about 787.

The Japanese, uncertain where the American blow would fall, had been unable seriously to oppose the American landings at Leyte; but they had prepared a plan to intervene as soon as possible afterwards. Their Fleet, following the disastrous Battle of the Philippine Sea, had had to split up. Most of the battleships and heavy cruisers had based themselves near Singapore and their sources of fuel oil, while the surviving aircraft carriers had returned to

Japan to get replacements of aircraft and air crews. These, in fact were not yet ready, and the plan had to take account of it.

On receipt of the order radioed by the C-in-C, Admiral Toyoda, from his headquarters in Japan, the various sections of the fleet were set in motion so as to arrive by separate routes off the Gulf of Leyte at dawn on 25 October. The main force, Force 'A' commanded by Admiral Kurita, was composed of five fast battleships, two of which, the *Yamato* and *Musashi,* were the largest and most powerful ships of their type in the world, each mounting nine 18-inch guns, twelve 6-inch and twelve 5-inch; nine heavy cruisers each mounting ten or eight 8-inch guns and tubes for launching their very effective 24-inch torpedoes; and fifteen destroyers with two light-cruiser leaders, all mounting 5-inch guns and a powerful torpedo armament.

Having refuelled at Brunei in North Borneo, this fleet set off following a route which was to take it to the west of Palawan Island to the Mindoro Strait and thence, threading its way between the lush green islands of the Philippines, through the Sibuyan Sea and San Bernadino Strait out into the Philippine Sea. There it would turn south round Samar to approach Leyte Gulf from the north and east.

Another group from Brunei was Force 'C' commanded by Admiral Nishimura – two older battleships, one heavy cruiser and four destroyers. This followed a route across the Sulu and Mindanao Seas to enter the Surigao Strait between the islands of Leyte and Mindanao, with orders to break through to attack the American landing fleet in the Gulf.

Following this squadron in support was another commanded by Admiral Shima,

Right:
This map shows the Japanese plan of attack and the American response to it.

composed of two heavy cruisers and four destroyers led by a light cruiser. Thus with Kurita's Force 'A', a giant pincer would close on Admiral Kinkaid's invasion fleet at Leyte. Having no carriers, these three forces would have to rely upon their big guns to attack the enemy ships and upon a combination of anti-aircraft gunfire and fighter planes from shore bases in the Philippines to give cover against attack by the aircraft from Halsey's carriers.

Finally there was the Carrier Force under Admiral Ozawa. Only a handful of planes with half-trained pilots being available, this was to be used as a decoy to lure away the American carriers of Task Force 38 and leave a clear passage for Kurita. For this purpose Ozawa steered from Japan for a position some 300 miles north of Halsey where he hoped to be discovered during the 24th.

All was now in train for the biggest naval battle in history.

Though it was air attack from the American carriers that the Japanese had most to fear, it was from quite a different element that the first blow came. Early on the morning of 23 October as Kurita in his flagship, the cruiser *Atago,* was leading Force 'A' up the west side of Palawan Island, torpedoes from the American submarines *Darter* and *Dace* sent the *Atago* and the cruiser *Maya* to the bottom and another cruiser, the *Takao,* limping back to Singapore. The Japanese admiral, picked out of the sea by a destroyer, transferred to the *Yamato;* Force 'A' meanwhile pressed on and early on the 24th was discovered entering the Sibuyan Sea by aircraft which had taken off from the decks of Carrier Group No. 2, operating off the San Bernadino Strait.

Admiral Fukudome, commanding the Japanese shore-based air fleet, had decided that the best way to give Kurita protection was by striking at Halsey's carriers rather than stationing his fighters defensively over the Japanese ships. Throughout that day Halsey's torpedo planes and bombers struck at Kurita, who looked up to the clear blue sky in vain for the expected fighter plane support.

By the end of the day the huge *Musashi* had gone to the bottom hit by many torpedoes, and the cruiser *Myoko* had been knocked out of action. The remainder of Kurita's fleet, after turning back for a time, resumed their course for the San Bernadino Strait when darkness brought them a respite, and during the night threaded their way through the narrow channel.

Fukudome's plan had certainly reduced the volume of attack on Kurita by forcing Carrier Group 3 to concentrate on self-defence. It had also cost Group 3 the carrier *Princeton* which, hit by a dive-bomber, was set furiously ablaze and had finally to be abandoned and sunk. But unless the plan to lure Halsey away worked, Kurita would have the full fury of the American carrier plane attack to face when day broke over the Philippine Sea as he emerged from the San Bernadino Strait.

It was not until the late afternoon that Halsey learned of Ozawa's fleet to the northward. He did not know that the Japanese carriers were 'paper tigers' so they at once became his primary target to destroy. By this time his returning flyers' reports had convinced him that Kurita had been so shattered that he was no great danger. The forces available to Kinkaid's Seventh Fleet and Halsey's No. 1 Group recalled from refuelling would be ample to

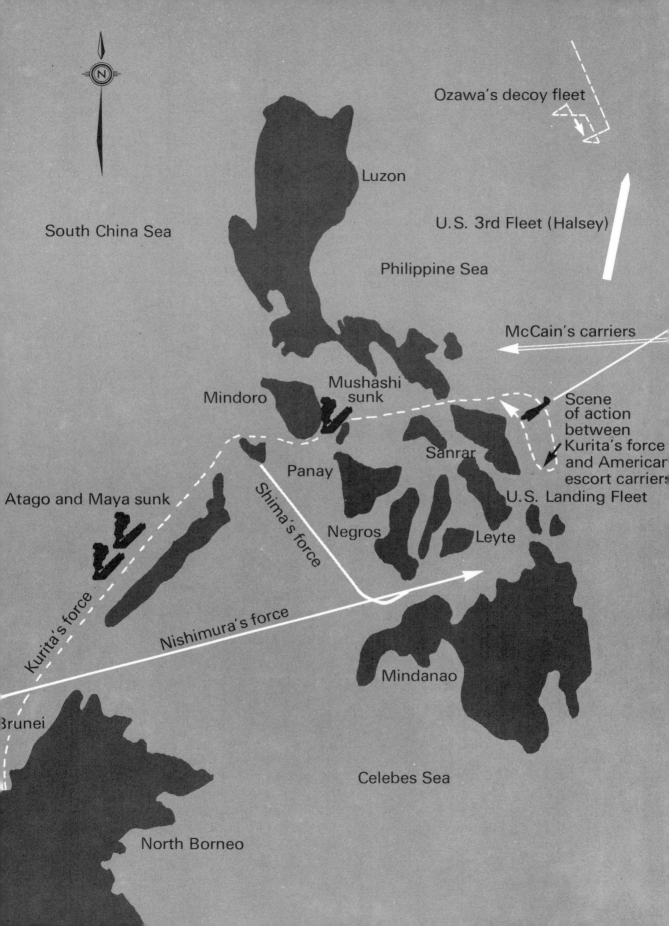

A scene from the Japanese attack on Sprague's carrier group. Sprague's gallant force was able to hold off Kurita's attack, until wearied by remorseless air attack, the Japanese commander left the chase and steamed away to join the *Yamato.*

deal with him, he thought. At midnight 24/25 October, therefore, Halsey set off to the north with his other three groups, determined to fall decisively upon Ozawa at dawn.

Unfortunately, not only was Kurita far from crippled, but through a signal mix-up, Admiral Kinkaid believed that Halsey had left a force composed of his six modern battleships and six cruisers off the entrance to the San Bernadino Strait, and he therefore took no precautions himself. The dire consequences of this mistake will be seen presently.

Meanwhile, as Halsey's powerful fleet was rushing away through the night just as the Japanese had planned, Nishimura's little squadron, followed at a distance by Shima's, was threading its way up the Surigao Strait. Their approach had been reported to Kinkaid and he had placed his forces to oppose them. At the southern entrance to the Strait, American motor torpedo boats working in pairs streaked in to the attack; but their only success was in damaging one of Shima's light cruisers. Nishimura, some 30 miles ahead of Shima, pressed bravely on to what he must have foreseen to be his doom, considering the great odds against him.

Next to attack him were destroyers belonging to the Seventh Fleet's bombardment group of battleships and cruisers under Rear-Admiral J. B. Oldendorf. He had spread his big ships across the exit from the Strait ready to bring their massive gunpower to bear on the advancing Japanese as soon as they came within range. In the meantime he released twenty of his destroyers which, guided by the 'magic-eye' of their radar detection instruments, advanced through the black tropical

night in small groups to launch their torpedoes from positions on either side of Nishimura's line.

The battleship *Fuso* and two Japanese destroyers were sunk; Nishimura's flagship, the battleship *Yamashiro,* was also torpedoed but pressed bravely on, being torpedoed three more times before going down under the storm of shells from Oldendorf's battleships and cruisers. The cruiser *Mogami,* heavily hit, and one destroyer were all that were left to turn to escape. When Shima, following up the Strait, saw the hopelessness of the situation, he also turned back. So one jaw of the pincer planned to crush the invasion force at Leyte had been broken off.

The other jaw, Kurita's Force 'A', thankful that with the setting of the sun the incessant attacks by Halsey's carrier planes had ceased, had meanwhile been passing through the narrow San Bernadino Strait as planned. When dawn broke he was off the east coast of the island of Samar. On the southern horizon could be seen the flat-iron shapes of aircraft carriers, already within range of his 18-inch and 14-inch guns. It was the northernmost of the three groups of escort carriers of the Seventh Fleet—taken completely by surprise and, it seemed, at Kurita's mercy.

The commander of the carrier group, Rear-Admiral Clifton Sprague at once flew off every available plane, many of them carrying unsuitable bombs or even depth-charges—there was no time to change to torpedoes—to do what they could to harass and delay the Japanese ships. The almost defenceless carriers then steered away for Leyte and the support of Oldendorf's battleships, at their utmost speed. This was only 18 knots—more than 12 knots less than that of their pursuers. As the tall splashes from Kurita's big guns leapt out of the sea round his ships, Sprague felt his squadron must surely be doomed.

But the gallantry of his airmen and of the six little escorts of his group who turned back and boldly attacked in the face of such heavy odds, worked an apparent miracle. Kurita's ships, swerving away to avoid torpedoes and suffering damage from bombs, were so delayed that more than two hours after the action had begun only one of the escort carriers had been sunk. In reply, four Japanese cruisers had been crippled or sunk; it had been at the cost of three of Sprague's escorts sunk and others damaged. Even so, by about 09.21 the remaining Japanese cruisers had got so close that the survival of the rest of Sprague's group seemed impossible: at that moment to the relief and amazement of all in the American ships, the enemy cruisers were seen to turn away and steam back to join the *Yamato*. Kurita, his confidence shattered by the ceaseless air attacks–which he believed came from Halsey's big carriers–had given up the chase.

After hesitating for some time he finally decided that he had nothing to gain by going on with the plan to penetrate to Leyte Gulf: he turned back to flee through the San Bernadino Strait to safety. The Seventh Fleet escort carriers were in fact to be made to suffer more heavily by a new form of attack–the *kamikaze* attacks by Japanese naval pilots from the airfields of Luzon, sworn to crash their bomb-laden planes suicidally on to enemy ships. Four of the carriers survived direct hits, though with heavy casualties and damage; but the *St. Lo* of Sprague's group blew up and sank.

While all this was going on, far away to the north Halsey's huge carrier force had caught up with and shattered Ozawa's decoy force, sinking all his carriers. Only two old battleships, two light cruisers and five destroyers escaped to Japan.

So the battle for Leyte Gulf ended: the Japanese had lost three battleships, four aircraft carriers, ten cruisers and nine destroyers as well as a great many planes. Furthermore almost every surviving Japanese unit had been damaged. It was the end of the Imperial Japanese Navy. The Allied fleet sailed unchallenged in the Pacific, except by air attack, for the rest of the war.

Figures in **bold** refer to
illustrations

Index

122